To Rena

Thank So Much for your Support. My prayer is that you take something about the way to heal from this book. ♡

Valerie Page

UNCOVER YOUR EYES TO ALLOW A DIVINE HEALING

Discover the Foreordained Pedagogy
Within Predestined Relationships!

✠ ✠ ✠

VALERIE PAGE

authorHOUSE®

AuthorHouse™
1663 Liberty Drive
Bloomington, IN 47403
www.authorhouse.com
Phone: 1 (800) 839-8640

Published by AuthorHouse 08/15/2017

ISBN: 978-1-5246-9515-6 (sc)
ISBN: 978-1-5246-9514-9 (e)

Library of Congress Control Number: 2017908652

King James Version (KJV)
Public Domain

CONTENTS

AUTHOR'S NOTE:

Where ever time allows you, take some personal timeout to reflect over your accomplished life journey. When a person stops to rewind their own individual steps of life, it becomes apparent how valuable the lessons and predestined people all are in our life journey. If you look closer through uncovered eyes, you will recognize how these blessings were intentional for our own spiritual growth. This story details a grieving Mother depicting her son's life journey while healing and releasing his legacy. My prayer is for God's favor, that his life story can lend a helping hand to anyone in need. The many lessons of life provided throughout these true experiences are for keener insight and wisdom of how vital God is. Happiness, disappointments, surprises, griefs, etc... are all tests to help make us stronger. It is very humbling to be granted the gift of choice. It is a gift that is powerful and when misused can be disastrous. The choices we make in life are critical in building a strong foundation. Imagine if you will, what it would be like to never have the gift of choice? These two years have been a very difficult process in writing this book and now I realize how much it helped me with my son's absence. The hard falls in life are necessary because they are intended for all to see what's really important! Don't allow the distractions to keep you from recognizing your purpose. It's an inheritance affixed from our youth and follows us into adulthood. With my co-Author, we commence the story at the exact moment my son (PJ's) life ended and bring it forward to honor his legacy. I've prayed long for guidance to arrive at its final print. As the Author along with PJ's spirit and all journals (both PJ's and mine) this experience continues to be a spiritual healing! The essential fibers that web this journey are all valuable lessons of Relationships!

Who we become derives from our personal environments, home-life, Church, School, etc. A parent's role is to consciously be attentive to the pressures of our youth which intensify daily. The cruelty of bullying along with other personality disorders has been a gradual plague with encroaching capabilities. Today it is highlighted through media just as PJ had predicted. To be born and raised by both parents, (Father & Mother) with standard morals is quietly diminishing. Whatever circumstances you're going through, I know from my own experiences, the best comfort and relief is found in the Bible! Growing up in my community I witnessed a host of refined spiritual Mothers, who took pride in setting the examples which fed positive influences to lots of children. A Father's role was also significant, teaching children lessons on how hard work and commitment could lead to financial success. My Mother's encouraging words were, "God makes no mistakes, and he made all of us". In spite of all bullying concepts I had her words to keep me holding my head up high. To have and sustain order in anyone's life is to include spiritual teachings, it can circumvent a lot of misconduct.

The practice of covering our eyes to the reality of truth, clamorously lives on today. There is nothing new under the sun! Will it ever fix itself? Identity is another pertinent concern today, many people still feel lost because they don't know their own history. When you look at the canvas of today's world you will find youth and adults still covering their eyes to the many facts concerning family history. Displaying PJ's story our family trees, still hold many covered details.. Factual information later in life can still give an emotional cleansing. God's word is vital and the understanding provides a survival kit for life. Staying true to yourself means, to maintain a spiritual, emotional and physical balance to stand on firm foundation. I highly recommend you grow with any form of spiritual education, it will enhance the rest of your life.

Uncovered Eyes Acknowledges True Blessings,….. Covered Eyes blind and block the intended lessons.

Obtaining my credentials as a license 'Relationship Educator' was strictly for my self-improvement. My certification is endorsed by 'Prepare and

Enrich Innovations' ((#1217906) Golden Hills) San Diego, CA, This experience was a high powered spiritual Bible Training that supplied great enlightenment for life experiences. A highly recommended self improvement prerequisite for all who value their self worth. You may ask, why? Communication skills provide much better insight to ensure lasting Relationships. This course assisted me with every type of Relationship, igniting growth in me to understand myself and others. The reward for me was identifying the improvements I needed, which in turn enhanced my Relationships of choice to last. Interacting with all the different connections of people require that you recognize the ones to invest in. Many evils lurk about us all wearing smiling faces and work hard to steal your joy. This Training brings out a clear spiritual and Biblical understanding for survival, but only when your eyes are uncovered. Relationships are necessary but you need clear eyesight to identify the ones predestined from God. "I can admit I have identified many intended lessons witnessing my son's journey." The time is now, let's all start uncovering our eyes to acknowledge what holds us hostage. Unmasking any pain you harbor will allow the healing to begin..............Rewind, Recall, Reveal & Release, the necessary prerequisites for Restoring the soul!

ACKNOWLEDGMENT

I acknowledge; My Family, my extraordinary Son (PJ), a loving husband and a host of great friends. Greatness comes from God of whom, I thank daily for the love of family (including all extended family). I couldn't have pushed forward in my pain without any of you. Special thanks to my husband who has been there for me through a lot of my trials and tests of faith. I thank my favorite Sister and her family, who continue to set great examples of family Love, Sacrifices and Strength for all to witness. I'd love to call you all out by name, but that would be endless. You all know who you are and I sincerely appreciate my God for allowing our paths to cross. My never ending prayers give me the assurance I needed in order to finally realize my Loss was instead, my Gain. My God is with me displaying daily how richly he continues to bless me.

If any one of you were ever moved to share your personal story, be encouraged, it may help others in need of hearing it. Our Purpose is to reach out and help someone else in life. It would be so powerful to reach the young and vulnerable early enough in life so they can grow in a positive light inspired to build new horizons. No One on this earth is without error? God purposely makes us all unique for a reason. Don't we all constantly Judge? Take a moment to reflect. Who are we to Judge another? Who do we become when we Judge others? Ask yourselves, who do we all pretend to be? How do others see us? Do we care? What truly are our biggest fears? Why did God grant us the privilege of life? There is only One True Judge and God has assigned us all uniquely with an individual purpose for being here. When you discover what your purpose is take immediate action to serve! Turn and help assist others. When you make the choice to serve be conscious to keep your eyes uncovered that you recognize the life lessons and the rewards! 'And we know that all things work together for good to them that love God, to them who are called according to his purpose.' Romans 8:28

God provides so many promises if only we follow his commandments.

"The liberal soul shall be made fat: and he that watereth shall be watered also himself". Proverbs 11:25

Look not at the things which are seen, but at the things which are not seen'. 2-Corinthians 4:16

Jean's testimony about her son, PJ's life, is filled with spiritual insight. The transparency of his purpose and the rewards his Mom (Jean) receives are simply divine. Jean's deceased Mother (Mae), a strong influence on their entire family, nurtured her children to grow and go with God shows the richness of being blessed with an impacting predestined Relationship. Mae's two daughter's (Jean and Rue) are still benefiting from all richness their Mother provided. Far too many people today give up on God's plan for family. The importance of Marriage first and then family were essential Relationships and it is what Mae wanted for her children. Jean's personal God driven purpose was exposed to her the minute her son was born. She remembers laying in her hospital bed immediately giving thanks to God for granting her the ability to have a healthy baby boy. Motherhood! This new experience brought the warmest spiritual love, joy and comfort. Jean held her son close to her heart remembering something her Mom had told her in her ninth month, "You will only experience the deepest true love once you have a baby", Yes! Jean felt it, Mom was Right! In spite of first husband (PJ's Dad), being at her bedside expressing the challenges that had taken over his entire body, Jean was still relieved she hadn't missed out on the opportunity of parenting. Jean could only focus on this new life and praying that as parents they could nurture PJ with sound wisdom and spiritual strength, just like her Mom had worked hard to raise her children. With all the colors of challenge showing around her even from her hospital bed, Jean was confident she would work hard to provide enough antidotes to circumvent the inevitable life challenges for them both. She knew her purpose was snuggled close to her heart and she felt overjoyed! "Thanks to God who makes all things possible. We should never assume we have endless time remaining, that is the boldest method to covering our eyes to reality. Even though PJ is out of sight he is with me in my heart for the rest of my life, his spirit rest deep within me. What a blessing to hold these treasures of memories in my possession, unobstructed, for the rest of my life. Hallelujah! Praise the Lord for opening my eyes to see my Gain! God blessed me with a needed spiritual heart transplant that happens when God becomes personal and comes to talk with you.

"UNMASKED THE HURT AND MEND YOUR HEART"! Rewind, Recall, Reveal, Release and you will Restore your spirit! I am honored to tell the amazing story to honor PJ's legacy. Putting these actual events down in book form continues to heal and restore my soul. Praises and Glory be to God.

The names have been changed to detail the story.

CHAPTER 1

REWIND *"OUT OF TIME"!*

It was the early morning on January 21, 2015 in cold Manhattan, New York, a predestined day Jean, will never forget. This was the day her only child, a son, was laid to rest at the Colombian Presbyterian Hospital. She'd never known the kind of chill that ran through her body, it was a terribly horrifying experience. Along with all the pain, Jean felt stunned, and recognized that there was no more time left to spend with her son, PJ. For any parent this has to be the worst rude awakening imaginable. Throughout PJ's thirty-five years, he ambitiously executed his dreams and his mother was the one rewarded, being chosen by God to fill that seat. The diagnosis by PJ's doctors was identified as pneumonia? But he had been unhooked from life support on the road to recovery, showing great signs of improvement. What the heck happened? The doctors had advised Jean, her son's young age was in his favor for a speedy recovery. This just couldn't be happening. PJ and his mom had made more future plans so recently that were still fresh on their lips. Jean just couldn't accept that PJ was gone, __ just like that. Her feelings of lifelessness made her so weak, it was the worst nightmare ever! Jean connected with the agony felt by so many parents who lose their children, she had no idea until now, what deep hurt felt like. Standing in the corridor with her husband, frozen and numb, her mind drifted off wondering about all the times in her life all the friends and family who dealt with life crises who she prayed for. Now her turn had arrived, unexpected and unannounced, so she had to be ready right now! The agonizing heart ache immediately attached itself to Jean's inner core and it was obvious this pain would last the rest of her life. PJ was gone! Jean just couldn't grasp the fact that just three days prior she was praying at PJ's bedside, he struggled to move his lips around the tubing trying to tell his mom, "I saw him." Jean trembled during that moment, PJ was trying to tell his mom, that he had seen God. Her tears spilled over uncontrollably as she continued describing how she felt that day, light headed, out of breath. The pain in Jean's heart made her entire body damp and she felt as though life was oozing out of her. Thank God, her husband was there to be of some comfort for her. He reached down to help Jean to her feet, more lessons popping into view, she saw with clarity the true tests of marriage. Jean's husband was predestined to be part of her life journey, he'd already experienced the same type of loss with one of his very own sons. Jean knew she had always thought selfishly being a single parent to one child. Both PJ and her had witnessed unappreciative family members and friends who chose not to honor their father and mother,... (Proverbs) Jean hadn't felt the desire to invest the time it would take for her to remarry and then have more children. She was selfishly focused on one child to ensure she could provide all that PJ needed. Jean also wanted to soar into a career of government logistics. It had never occurred to her that is was possibile for PJ to be laid to rest before her. Instead, Jean's concentration was set on equipping PJ with suitable knowledge for the probable encountering of his approaching peer pressures. With humility, Jean put forth efforts in doing her best to set an example for her son. All of these thoughts coming to view were just her search for the fuel she needed to get through the pain of missing PJ. She witnessed her mother go through many trials, and that strength was the fuel Jean held on to tightly. Through many lives around us we can see tragedy but we never consider it can become our own. A light came on from just recapping her mom's life. Another life lesson. PJ's early maturity was driven by a force to be reckoned, he spiritually turned into this little confident man as though he already knew his purpose! Clinging tight fisted, to one of PJ's recent pictures, Jean kept expressing her gratitude for God's blessings to have placed PJ in her life. She had to grip the reality that PJ was gone from her. She heard her Mother's soft words feeding her heart while she retrieved those precious days spent with PJ. God gives the increase, it could have all ended with only a call_ and no time left to spend!

Another reckoning for Jean, was realizing it was God's order. It was clear now, why she had been encouraged to go back and check on her home life and her husband. Even though it all felt highly stressful to bring her sick husband back to New York, it was all in God's master plan. We should never under estimate the order intended;

Jean says, she still gets choked up realizing how many ways things happened to show God's work with every inch of their life through___ and all the way to PJ's home going celebration. Jean observed a mended and transformed husband comforting her in every way. He had become her anchor; ready, willing and now able to help her with every detailed matter. Only God gives the increase! Being married thirteen plus years definitely brings about challenges, but Jean's awakening says. "It's really not about the trivial matters of marriage, so uncover your eyes to see clearly the reasons you keep your vows and know Love is always the answer to give to one another for the storms and heart breaks of life will come. When a man and woman become one through marriage it's to hold each other up at all times! And that is not saying it will be easy!"

The second trip back, Jean and her husband stayed in Times Square near the subway station. Jean wants to rewind a bit to recap the previous week when she first arrived at the hospital, how she ran down the hall into her sister's arms, surrounded by PJ's team of doctors. It was as if she were walking through a dream down white hallways, seeing only her sister at the end of the hall with open arms, she remembered all the white coats in the hallway with Rue all moving their lips but she hears no words. Sometimes, when in shock, our eyes become covered to everything happening around us and we hear nothing. Jean indicates that her own mother and father's passing kept her buffering a numbness by focusing only on the preparations for funeral services. At that moment she didn't know nor could she even imagine how she was going to get through this chapter of her life,___unbelievable pain! Jean wants to unravel, she remembered standing with her eyes closed tight, it felt as if PJ and her mother Mae were close at her side, but when she opened her eyes, it was her husband standing there. It is God's assurance. Yes, God is always providing for his children. Over and over her agonizing thoughts kept reoccurring, because both men in her life were simultaneously being critically challenged. The discernment hit Jean like a ton of bricks, this was her complete immediate family! Jean's headaches were repetitive, she had been praying without ceasing. Right in front of her (covered) eyes her prayers had already been answered. Jean's state of mind was filled with distractions, she hadn't noticed how tremendous her husband's health had improved. Granted, Jean had plenty reason for being inattentive. Finally they were on the plane ride for the return trip back to N. Y. hospital and Jean wants to already be there. Rewinding, she visualized her Mother's face and heard a very faint voice in her ear "I prayed that man up for you!" Jean shivered at the realization her husband's health was like new; he had a second wind. Jean had been praying her son would have the same renewing. "He healeth the broken in heart, and bindeth up their wounds." (Psalm 14:3) The three day turn around went as planned, Jean couldn't exhale, and she just wanted to get back to PJ's side. They were just about to board the last plane from the layover and her cell phone started ringing. The doctors were calling and this time it wasn't good news, Jean's expression made that clear. This time the doctors were saying, that PJ's pneumonia symptoms were striking back again, PJ was once more, back on life support. This call brought on instant anxiety. Jean had been elated to bring PJ back home, no matter what it required. An alarm went off in her head. All of the previous reports of positive changes in PJ had caused her to relax with her consistent prayers. Again she had covered her eyes to this awareness. Jean began to tearfully pray, asking first, for forgiveness of her short comings. In her talk with God she confessed her guilt when life was good that she had fallen short in her Christian practices. Jean began again praying long and hard about everything and everybody, also how grateful she was for her husband's recovery. Jean kept her head down for most of the plane ride. Her stomach was in knots! Sitting there sick with pain, Jean pulled up all of Pasha's earlier texts, comfort to read, revealing all the attentive check-ins concerning PJ's earlier conditions when Jean had gone back to California (Ca). With a serene heart, Jean silently continued praying.

All the texts from family responding to her earlier messages about PJ's improvements were heartbreaking for Jean. She had previously told a few folks, how PJ was sitting up, eating ice and all the oxygen tubes had been removed and all was good. Almost 2 weeks of progress and now PJ was back to square one, he could not breathe on his own anymore. Jean cried with excruciating pain, wondering if this was because of her slackness in praying. Jean knew she had to get a grip, remembering, it's always in God's order. "For with God nothing shall be impossible." (Luke 1:37)

Jean and her husband finally made it to the hospital and at the time intended, as they walked thru the corridors, she privately felt a painful disconnect. It was only a matter of seconds, PJ had just floated into a peace filled sleep, set free of all his discomforts. God had called this warrior home. At that moment Jean couldn't feel anything, no outward display of hysteria, it was happening, the 'Peace that surpasses all understanding' took control of Jean's presence, providing her unusual comfort. She knew that God had decided it was time for PJ to return to his rightful home with no long suffering prescribed. Thank God, Jean also had her spiritual shoulder to lean on. "God is our refuge and strength, a very present help in trouble." (Psalm 46:1) God's words kept surfacing from study "Him that over cometh will I make a pillar in the temple of my God" (Rev 3:12) She kept saying, "It is not about Jean, it's about the peace that PJ now has!" Had it not been for God's order, sending family out ahead, positioning the fabulous team of doctors and Ms. Pasha to assist her all with their purposes to serve, Jean would've been a basket case. With her eyes uncovered, Jean envisions, all the cherished days spent being at PJ's bed side, cognizant of how God had extended PJ's time so they both could have his ending days together! Amazing! Jean's Restoration, was all already planned way ahead of time by God. Jean will never forget their time to hold hands, for unspoken lovingly lingering looks, witnessing his improvements, time for kisses, tears and prayers together. Hallelujah! What gifts! It could have all just ended without these opportunities. Jean acknowledges the abundant blessings from all the rewinding and looking with uncovered eyes. PJ's progress was induced by the predestined team of doctors, PJ had the best care and he was placed at the best reputable hospital in Manhattan. These were all significant parts of a divine master plan laid out since PJ's birth, how amazing is that! PJ knew his Step Dad was sick and kept trying to tell his Mom to go home and be strong. Jean had even suspected then that PJ was trying to tell her to be more worried about Step Dad. It's almost impossible to put into words the magnitude of weight and agony Jean carried with her worrying about her two significant loved ones while contemplating what to do next. Witnessing both of their challenges simultaneously Jean was stunned to realize how drastic her life could become. Her only choice was to turn it all over to God, because 'Only God can give the increase'. Jean's repetitive quote for years had been, "It's not about me", now she felt it with enormous impact! The visible proof of how powerful God's love stretches, was proven with what her family and friends both near and far, provided her through the tough days that followed. Jean testifies about all the continued love powering through from New York, Texas, Arizona, Nebraska, Florida, Alabama, Georgia, Tennessee, Hawaii, Virginia, S. Carolina, California, Dominican Republic and San Lucia all to celebrate PJ's life. It was evident that when you can touch peoples lives, the results will show in many ways. Jean understood a particular spiritual message she's kept close at heart. It's entitled 'Footprints In The Sand', her tears connected with discernment. So many thoughts surfaced from rewinding, Jean clearly knew every time God had carried her. To this present day Ms. Pasha and Jean are still bonded friends for life. The closure in New York was very hard, it took 4 days for all matters to conclude. PJ's extended family were awesome. During their stay in New York, Jean caught a very bad case of Flu virus. Snow was heavily falling everywhere, and the news media was informing all travelers of air flight cancellations. Jean was so grateful to look up to see her husband providing all of their needs for their continued stay. Everything required was resolved in such a way you knew it was all blessed by God. Jean was drained, sick and sad, she could not leave the hotel bed for 2 whole days. Jean says, "Thanks be to God for blessing me back into good health. Every thing we are able to do is never our doing, Thank you God."

Jean called her Aunt Cil, a strong Christian woman by example, who could calmly get the word out to all the family that PJ had passed. Aunt Cil, had the spiritual make up to receive PJ's passing as a comfort and not a tragedy, she knew God's teachings very well. Aunt Cil was one of the strategically placed people in Jean's life. Whenever Jean petitioned for any help needed, she mindfully acknowledged who was making it all possible, Every response to all her requests were full of love and so ready and willing to help. Jean's eyes were still uncovered, no way could she miss the comprehension of this amazing lesson from God.

PJ is now with our Lord and Savior to rest in eternity. Jean always loved taking pictures of PJ's every involvement and so happy she followed her heart because all these pictures helped to restore and reconstruct her whole being. This is where she spends quiet time before and after prayer time most days.

It is a huge treasure for Jean, recapping numerous endless memories, on film and in numerous on-line files. Taking, keeping and saving pictures are Priceless.

Jeans's prayer is in hopes that this book may encourage anyone's curiosity and thirst for the Bible. Introduce yourself to the stories of the Bible, you will want to share them. It can arouse a desire to study more. The Bible is where you can find answers about everything in life. With regular study, you can better prepare yourself to receive blessings abundantly. Being uneducated and without God's word can make life so much harder. If you feel like something is missing in your life, try this on! It won't erase our fate but it is a necessary tool for survival while we live. You may even dissect and use this story in your bible classes.

It's been two years since the passing of PJ, and every new day Jean acknowledges her gratitude for the improved insight of God's preserved plan for her life. Jean thought she would never ever feel alive again after PJ died, but she is constantly reminded of many things shared between them, one being, "Mom, If you're Okay, I'm Okay"! Most quotes mentioned here came from particular books she once gifted PJ with. Jean's daily practice is counting her blessings one-by-one. Jeans testifies that once you practice doing this you will discover when you go beyond 10 or even 20 blessings this will substantiate how richly God blesses you! The numerous rewinds of PJ's journey, helps Jean understand how PJ had been preparing her for his own home going all of his growing years. Jean's eyes were covered during her earlier Single Parenting years, and it caused her to stumble and fall a lot, missing the real spiritual lessons intended. But this was already in the plan in order for Jean to grow, and God kept working on her with his unconditional love. It is astounding to recognize that our Lord and Savior already knows about all the events and order of all our individual daily walks from beginning to end. It is better that only God knows our fate, because as human beings we really couldn't handle the truth! Jean is reminded in her life journey how she found out truths about her own childhood which could have badly damaged her if she had learned about it to soon. It was revealed only at the ordained time intended. She admits while in her adolescence, she may not have accepted it. Thank the Lord, for aligning it with God's timing and not our own. Jean laughs out loud, "It's amazing how we all put so much effort into concealing things from others when God sees it all."

"Let your conversation be without covetousness; and be content with such things as ye have: for he hath said, I will never leave thee, nor forsake thee." Heb 13:5

Jean pauses with deep thought, "My pain is still so raw and the memories will continually be recounted, I pray to God to help me every step of the way and grant his favor to help me to keep my eyes uncovered now. I also pray that all PJ's extended family and friends heal with me. Uncover your eyes and discover your many blessings. The results are great enlightenment. It will set you free."

CHAPTER 2

RECALL (Three Weeks Earlier,... how it evolved)

The 4th day of January 2015, is when PJ, collapsed in his New York home with his extended family close at hand. They moved and reacted acted with urgency. His Dominican family were home with him and rushed him to one of the best hospitals in Manhattan by emergency ambulance. PJ adopted into this family in 2005. They are who Jean had come to love for being a part of PJ's life, and they were quick to contact Jean to tell her as best they could, what happened. Jean needed a translator because like PJ, they were all fluent in Spanish. Jean was very proud that PJ had learned Spanish in his youth because she knew it would give him life opportunities. He had always been Jean's Spanish interpreter, and constantly encouraging his mom to learn the language too. You can't imagine how blank and disoriented Jean felt with all this coming on her all at once, she knew she needed to stay sane and not panic! Just like that, no warning! Simultaneously a specific circle of lives were instantly changed. Jean and her husband were living in Ca when they received the call that P J was in the hospital, grabbing at her chest, her heart pain was crazy, it was such a shock. Her first thought was evident, God has all control and the test of faith was now in her lap, her prayers were what she clung to in hopes that all be okay. It was unbelievable news! Jean and PJ had just talked a week earlier and he said nothing about feeling sick. She listened to the young Dominican boy of PJ's extended family speaking in English but what she was hearing was all so unimaginable to Jean. It was every parent's nightmare. Jean tried to describe her feelings, being gut wrenching, incredible knock-out pain that made her unsteady. It was all too much for Jean, she understood now more than ever what it meant to fall to your knees. Jean's entire body felt weak and her head ached and she felt as though she would stop breathing any second. Through the phone she kept hearing those words, "PJ in Hospital, PJ needs help! You need to come now, PJ's on Life Support! The Doctor will Call You! Oh My! What? NO!, not possible. What the heck happened?! How? Jean just knew she was going to wake up from a nightmare dream, but, that never happened. Through tear stained eyes she looked up to see that her husband was standing right at her side and realized God's gifts were prevalent a reminder to keep her eyes uncovered. She saw the significance of having this husband who personally identified with her new experience. Even though it hurt her heart to the core, this was proof up front that God was the master planner revealing who was in control. Appreciative for her Mother who had instilled a strong thirst for God's word during the beginning stages of her Motherhood, Jean knew it was now her time for suffering just as the bible prepares us. Her pain let out a cry that could be heard for miles, her words were "I do know what it means to truly Trust, Believe and sincerely Pray" Jean couldn't concentrate or think straight and in her mind she continued allowing scriptures to surface. "Let us therefore come boldly unto the throne of grace, that we may obtain mercy, and find grace to help in time of need." Heb 4:16 "The lord also will be a refuge for the oppressed. A refuge in times of trouble." (Psalm 9:9) Jean reflects on the times that she spent encouraging other people during their trials, always being guided through her heart to say comforting words. Now that it was her turn to feel the sufferings, she really needed a mountain of encouragement, all while realizing she didn't really even want to talk at all right then_not while her feelings were freshly tearing her insides apart. It wasn't possible, the pain was just so big_"He knoweth the way that I take: when he has tried me, I shall come forth as gold". (Job 23:10)

With unending tears, Jean cries out, "Oh Father God, the pain is so deep"! The house phone starting ringing causing Jean to jump, her nerves were on edge, they both saw New York on caller ID. It was PJ's assigned team of specialist, calling to explain what they had observed from all of their examinations. More alarming information was making Jean tremble all over, PJ had been in the hospital two days already? What?? One of his lungs had become fully infected which resulted from earlier mistaken diagnosis of flu and cold-like symptoms and as a result PJ had not been treated for the real culprit, which they now identified as Pneumonia. New York's fierce winters was all Jean could surface hearing this.

During this phone call the doctors continued explaining the lack of oxygen to his lungs had caused major malfunction of his heart. This is what brought PJ to the point of collapsing at his New York home. Jean identifies another blessing, PJ was at his home with family when he collapsed. Thank God! She continues listening to the doctors, while subconsciously going over her most recent conversations with PJ,_the doctor's voice became a whisper in the background revisiting months earlier when PJ made mention of a cold/flu like symptoms which he assured her were normal occurrences during New York's winter months. PJ had been screened by his primary doctor who'd given him antibiotics. Those results convinced him just as he assured Jean there was nothing to worry about. Being humorous PJ even added that he had on his flip flops like he always wore in Ca living by the beach. He loved to make jokes a lot just like his Dad. In spite of his young age the doctors kept saying PJ's heart was being challenged, but why? She remembered now that PJ's Dad had heart trouble too, but his reasons were brought on from an abusive life style of drugs. Jean drifted off into long deep thoughts, _ when and if they weren't visiting with each other in person they would communicate regular by texts, emails, or just phone calls, talking weekly/bi-weekly. Their long talks would always conclude with Jean asking PJ, if there were any particulars he needed or wanted. There were so few times that he would accept gifts from his Mom. He was a proud young man, always displaying the responsible strong man image and persistent with Jean that all things were good! PJ would always hang up with telling Jean not to worry so much. She retraces her texts to him the last few days had no immediate responses which meant it was time for a phone call just to hear his voice. She had always dreaded PJ's move, putting too many miles between him and all his immediate family, but Jean respected his choice and understood why he aspired to find his own place in life. Every single day Jean missed PJ and he knew exactly how painful it was for his Mom, he knew how and when to pacify her with phone calls, pictures, gifts along with several projected travel plans for them and Jean admits the timing was always on point. Everyone who truly knew PJ (neighborhood, Church, College, Co-Workers, Mom's employees) admired him for his logic, directness and genuinely appreciated his outspoken intellect. His attention to detail and initiative to know any subject well, especially before ever speaking on it, was his meticulous persona, it was his signature! PJ's vast knowledge of the Bible and the gifted clarity, in which he comprehended it, had many thinking he would one day be called to minister. Although PJ said he never felt that calling, once he relocated to New York, it didn't take long before he had offers from the church he attended petitioning for PJ to teach young men and woman's Bible study. Jean knew from PJ's early age that he was exceptional. Jean with her mother Mae prayed PJ would be appreciated for his talents and not envied for his gifts. She recalls the exact situation that commenced during PJ's grieving adolescence to compound the worse growing pains imaginable. They all witnessed the cruelty of how bullying began to steal PJ's joy. This was a time that Jean admits she was trying to rationalize, justify, or maybe even classify it as being misread. All of which were not accurate and a bad move for Jean to make. In all actuality it was disheartening for Jean to discover who all the participants were with this mistreatment; church people, school classmates, adult haters, and even some family members. Jean remembers how much she didn't want to believe it, she had clouded her vision, thinking these people liked both her and PJ. No one took time to know what he was going through nor cared. Jean, like her mom, wanted to believe people were good more than they were not. To discover her own faults, one being always covering her eyes, caused Jean to miss a few of her intended life lessons. Jean really needed to pull herself together and get to the hospital in New York immediately. Cognizant that PJ was on life support, she had to make decisions and move fast! Jean trusted that God would carry her through all that she had to do and she felt the guidance of her mother close by. Just like that, she had an instant plate of life's inevitable struggles compounded! Just a few months prior to the news about PJ, Jean was very shocked about her husband's health. PJ had been checking in with his mom on a regular basis asking about Step Dad's health. She pondered, wondering if PJ knew about a challenged then and didn't want to worry his Mom? Jean never considered anything like this to happen. The first thing she did was drop to her knees in prayer. The abundance of emotions hit her like a ton of bricks. Jean knew to keep telling herself, God makes no mistakes as he rules over all our lives!

Jean's mom had been her comforter for all past situations, mother Mae was always genuinely ready to receive, listen and comfort her children through all their circumstances. Through prayers Jean surfaces more blessings, her mother's wisdom, what a gift! She went on explaining how her mom's wishes were always for her to settle down and with an older man. She felt Jean needed someone who loved the Lord and had self worth to meet her progressiveness. Jean's new husband and momma Mae had a great connection from the start which in turn materialized a special bond. So to have her husband right by her side, allowed Jean to feel her mom's presence too. When the call from the hospital came through, Jean's husband was still right there ready to comfort and assist her. How great God's timing and order of events are. Jean confesses, the man she married also had a genuine understanding of this same type of crisis, it would have been so much harder to have this experience any other way. Jean repetitively expresses her spiritual gratitude, she perceives the volume of blessings in sorting and unfolding PJ's life. The best medicine for all pain, is already in our possession, just uncover your eyes to heal.

Jean prepares herself to make the call to her favorite sister, her one and only sister, another blessing she'd appreciated her whole life. Jean's prayers were answered when she was 13 years old growing up with three brothers which had always made her want a sister. God blessed her family with a baby sister, right on time. Jean's sister (Rue) has always been an incredible Aunt for PJ's growing years, and when it came time for Jean to tackle single parenting, Rue was always right there to help in every way. God's ordained order never merits questioning! Jean's tears are all over the pages of this book, it is in God's order that two plus years after PJ's call home this book is finally in the closing stages. Jean with her hands held high up towards the heavens, says her tears are now filled with joy! "Rejoice evermore. Pray without ceasing. In everything give thanks: for this is the will of God in Christ Jesus concerning you". (1 Thess 5:16-18) Jean did not want to impose her husband with any travel at that time because of his health and it was crucial that she get to New York, like yesterday. Realizing her husband's humility from losing his own son, she again became filled with emotions, men camouflaged and reserve their sufferings more than women. She realized through more prayers she really wanted him to get well and keep that strong shoulder for her to lean on. Trying her hardest to be firm and persuade her husband she would be fine, she sucked in a big breath, pulled up her big girl pants, and booked the first flight out the following morning. Packing in zombie mode, she grabbed her Bible, the gift card box from her brother and sister'n'law, plus three easy access photos just to look at him during the flight. Continuing in her mode she packed a mid size suitcase for January weather in New York. Jean did it all in such haste and not aware at the time of all the essentials for that climate. Her focus was also to ensure her husband had all he needed in her absence. "Yea, though I walk through the valley of the shadow of death, I will fear no evil: for thou art with me." (Psalm 23:4)

That night before leaving out Jean knew she had to call Rue. Finally, she had her sister on the phone. Once Jean heard her voice over the phone she felt the unraveling begin. She tried hard to get the words out about PJ and then it all came up in her throat and out in garble. The next thing her sister heard was Jean's drowning cries which caused her to blurt out uncontrollably PJ's condition and soon they were both hysterical. Once they both collected themselves enough to talk, her sister Rue turned it around to comforting Jean. "Sis, if there's anything I can do, you tell me, name it"! Right away, Jean felt some of her weight lift, and her unstable feelings defused a bit. Real love is so monumental, Jean knew her love for her son had stood the test of time because of all the miles apart for so many years. If only their momma Mae were living, Jean lost in the moment pictured how even during such perplexity, the three of them together would exude great strengths. "But my Mom (through God) gave me life and an awesome sister who was ready, willing, and able, she was a mini replica of momma Mae." Before taking off for the airport, Jean could now give her husband some comfort telling him that family would be meeting her in New York. Jean remembers how committed her sister and niece were, immediately preparing to get there the very same day. God is so Great!

Jean's sister already had huge responsibilities of her own, so she conversed with other family members who did their part to help out during her absence. What a comfort! The blessings were pouring. Jean still concerned about her husband's current health condition, blindly selected a return date of 8 days, which was subject to change. Jean's over whelming pain was uncontrollably dominating her every move, but Jean assured her husband she would call him regularly. With that, she headed out for the airport, praying to God to watch over both her men. She also prayed for God's favor to get her to New York ASAP without winter weather deterrents. Focusing on continued prayers assisted her with renewed faith and courage. Her emotions were compiling again, even with the layover it felt like the longest plane ride of her life. Jean kept trying to understand the direction of God's order, she knew it was a test. She was in flight and the altitude, the emotional and air turbulence were all consuming her entire body, she began to feel nauseous, she did not panic but chose to compose herself with continued prayer. She continued her focus by surfacing on a lot of scriptures; "God so loved the world that he gave his Only begotten son, that whosoever believes in him shall not perish but have everlasting life" (John 3:16) Jean cried silently most of her flight, identifying with the enormous sacrifice God made for us all. Wow! The new impact and realization of it's meaning to her was also as he'd planned. She thanked God for the ability to analyze and absorb this hard lesson. As much as she had quoted that scripture, never did it have this impact. She realized the sacrifice God had made for all people to live in a world of great sin. So many mothers have lost an only child, (young / old) and young children have lost their parents and the list of dieing goes on endlessly. Jean uncovered her eyes and asked herself, "Who am I to think I should rate such pardon,_ my son already belonged to our heavenly Father and has been on loan to ME! Her gratitude intensified that her mother had raised her up grooming her to become a God fearing parent. Jean was enriched with feelings gone by of her attentive routine with early Bible studies. It is what prompted her thirst for more of God's word. She was especially grateful she was chosen by God to be the mother of such an extraordinary son. These were the kind of talks she had with herself throughout the long flight. She held on tight to faith putting all her focus on prayer with anticipation that all was going to be fine. This began calming her spirit and building her strength again, she had to be strong for the work awaiting her in New York. Jean needed to be ready to show her trust and faith as soon as she laid eyes on PJ, no matter what the circumstances. Recalling the many life events with PJ from childhood to now, recapping so many happy times fueled her with Love and brought smiles to her face. Aside from PJ's summer and spring visits to Ca, Jean brought to mind how his Step Dad and her would try to persuade PJ to come to Ca (their treat) during the fall seasons so he could enjoy the Ca sun! All the Ca family could see the rough weather reports in New York during the fall and winter with jokes on weather comparison. On one occasion when PJ came home to Ca, friends and family all drove to Arizona just to show PJ plans of retirement life and to see if warmer climate would at least spike his interest to come back. PJ would say the real reward was just having quality family time with his Mom, family and friends of choice. Some visits he would emphasize that he only wanted to see his mom and plans of his own agenda. Jean recalls PJ joking with her about their retirement home location while admiring Step Dad's vision and mindset for the future. PJ joked about how the floor plan included hallways that were spacious and wide for wheel chairs. He could always make his mom laugh out loud. Knowing his mom was people oriented he just had to ask "What will you find to do in the desert"? She remembers how they both laughed hard and loud.

As Jean sat looking out the window of the plane finally starting to see land down below, she was thinking and feeling the joy of convincing PJ to move back to Ca. She even thought she could aggressively insist! Her thoughts helped to replace her anguish with soothing and positive feelings as she prepared for the plane's layover to change planes. As everyone sat waiting for the signal to leave the plane she look around at blank stares and wondered how many people had heavy laden hearts for their trips to New York.

Leaving the plane, Jean walked out in zombie motion, wishing she was already in New York. In her heart the message was clear, keep your eyes on the prize, Jean had to remember there will always be an order to how God gives the increase and in his timing. She kept telling herself, just 'Let Go and Let God!' "These things I have spoken to you, that in Me you may have peace, In the world you will have tribulation, but be of good cheer, I have overcome the world". (John 16:33) "God is our refuge and strength, a very present help in trouble."(Psalm 46:1) Retrieving memories of how she use to nag PJ about living so far away, what if he got sick and needed her, his reply was, "Mom, if I ever get sick while I'm living in N. Y., I wouldn't want you to know because you would be on the first thing smoking, and once you got there, What could you do?" Jean grabbed at her heart pounding hard. PJ moved first to Florida, hurricane country, and their Monday morning talks would be just that, what if anything happened and he needed her. Jean insisted that they have weekly talks when he first moved, to comfort her and they talked about all topics, especially the family buzz. Jean missed him so much and wanted him to be apart of all family matters. PJ had been her rock, he'd continued to help his mom even long distance with updated technology, never imagining she would be caring for and assisting him for his every need. Jean was so ready to do whatever PJ's needs would require. At the layover, her cell phone started blowing up. The information about PJ on life support was slowly getting out to all the family and close friends. Numerous incoming texts and calls were mounting, all with concerns and questions. Of course Jean was still in shock and too emotional to talk. Up until now, she'd never appreciated the value and significance of texts and caller ID. Now only with prioritization, Jean began answering a few of the calls by texts only. These are the times when the discovery is made of which people are gifted with great bedside manner minus all the rest. Inescapable tears and prayers were Jean's entire layover. Waiting out the layover, Jean reminisced on more of her mother's teachings on great spiritual insights. Jean's early guidance were something she apparently absorbed with her eyes uncovered. Seeing so clear how her mom's consistent spiritual application caused greatness for their family. This actually brought smiles to Jean with tears flowing, thinking how her next book would be about her Mom's commitment to God and family. It is what helped Jean learn early to trust in God. Jean endlessly recapped

Biblical scriptures, writing them all down, because in her hast to leave home she left her Bible in the car. "The Lord is nigh unto them that are of a broken heart and saveth such as be of a contrite spirit." (Psalm 34:18) Jean walked through the Airport she was moved to stop and buy a book in one of the gift shop, and she spotted one entitled 'Phone Calls from Heaven'. She could, now, board the plane again a bit more revitalized with a book to refocus and refuel herself. Jean began reading about the phone calls from heaven, she assumed she needed to apply all of these same nurturing phrases to her very own heartache. Hearing her mother's voice in her ear, "God gives us no more than we can handle" the message was clear,... whatever this leads to, just be ready to handle it! Jean pondered, where was this new chapter of life taking them? Never, ever had she felt weight of this magnitude, it hurt so bad! The positive rejuvenated feelings were sinking fast and she was back in a mountain of tears. This time when Jean's phone rang, it was her adopted daughter acquired from her professional career before retirement. Jean had bonded with this beautiful young military worker because both their moms had passed away during the same time. Relationships! Jean answered this call for it was right on time, like in the book she was reading. Amazing! It was Miss Moe who was like a daughter to Jean before, during and long after her retirement. They stayed in contact and at this very perfect timing, she was calling. Moe was stationed in Norfolk VA, but this call was right on time, a call Jean could answer, a call from heaven, Wow! Thank you God! She felt blessed and spared but humbled by her predestined journey. Jeans thoughts were, "keep me humble, dear Lord, when I am faced with undeserved problems". "Be not afraid neither be thou dismayed: for the Lord thy God is with thee whithersoever thou goest." (Josh 1:9)

Influenced by her great Aunt Nie, Jean had always busied herself with outreach volunteer work at nursing homes. Working to serve others out in the field was what Jean found so rewarding.

Jean switched and reflects back to PJ's first close family death, his Dad. At that time Jean recalls her prayers of favor for PJ to see God's significant order with his eyes uncovered to include discernment.

The test of faith increasingly enlightened them both of God's word and they used that repellent as a shield of armor for life's circumstances. PJ had grown up with better clarity of God's teachings than many young adults his age, plus he already knew a few things about his Dad's challenges. Jean thought about how she would pray for God's hand to keep PJ shielded from the many influences of his Dad's life style. She also saw the lucidity of why she continued to limit her conversations to PJ about his Dad. Looking now through uncovered eyes, Jean could see it may have not been the best choice for a growing young man, but she'd already made the choice. After his Dad passed, more deceased family members crowded the canvas. It was devastating for a young man just approaching his teens witnessing his Dad's family ties of benevolence become indifferent while burring the deceased. We have to learn to stop suppressing emotional feelings and instead, learn to let them go. Who ever leaves behind a sweet fragrance in your life, acknowledge that God blessed you to have that gift. You never lose someone, if you know where they are. Release your pain(s) and began the healing process, it only works with time. Keep your eyes uncovered so you don't miss the lessons of life, it is the only way to push forward. The time had come for Jean to experience what suffering really means! She prayed sincerely whatever PJ's condition would be, she wanted to be strong and not fall apart in front of him. All she wanted now was for him to return back home to Ca with her.

Fast forwarding to her arrival at Colombian Presbyterian Hospital in Manhattan, New York. This trip was not like the other exciting trips to New York to see PJ. January was just like they show on the news, very wet, dreary cold atmosphere with snow everywhere. After the shuttle bus let her out in front of the hospital, she had to determine which one of the very tall hospital buildings PJ was in. Rue and family were already there. They had left after Jean yet managed to arrive to New York before her. This is where you can see God's order take over. Jean was unaware of all the deterrents while in her state of mind, but it was a giant blessing that she had finally made it. Bombarded with so much stuff, Jeans hands were full with suitcase and coats to last several weeks. Jean was finally in the right place, out of breath, headed up the elevator, still covered with layers of spiritual food. The door of elevator opened, her destination was down the hall. In all the cold she felt her forehead breakout in perspiration as her heart raced. The very first person she laid eyes on was her favorite sister Rue, so soothing to her eyes, the right buffer before seeing PJ. Jean knew she had done right to spiritually refresh herself the instant she saw Rue's face! This is the time when Jesus carried Jean. She knew right then that she had to be stronger now than ever before in her life. Every bit of her religious beliefs had to be a strong hold. She could see the strength in her Christian Grandmother, mom and Aunt whom she witnessed growing up and how courageous they were during these inevitable times. A voice in her head said, "You must be very strong and turn up the mommy skills and get to PJ's bed side." (It was momma Mae). She was greeted by his team of doctor's all talking and looking concerned as they greeted Jean. She remembered hearing those same voices over the phone and now she was right there with them with anticipation to see PJ. The doctor's voices became very faint and distant. Jean felt Rue's hand pushing her past doctors and right to the door of PJ's room. Jean floated towards the room where PJ lay anticipating their union. Once PJ saw his mom, there was no stopping their embrace. PJ held up his arms trying to motions for his mom to come closer and Jean moved as fast as a zombie mode person could. PJ was hooked up to so many tubes, but for that moment in time, it didn't matter. Their embrace locked them together indefinitely. When she finally stood up and saw the surroundings more clearly, immediately, Jean wanted desperately to rearrange the entire scene in that hospital room.

Her first thought was to stay composed and not let PJ see his mom fall apart. Jean wanted to display big hope and confidence that all was going to get better. Again she focused on her mom and Aunt Cil the way they carried bountiful faith in crisis and it comforted her. Jean held on to PJ as best she could, aware of the importance of all the connecting tubes. Jean was humbled to finally be there by his side, she began to comfort him with her motherly nurturing, telling him he was going to be fine. PJ had lots of facial expressions and if you knew him you could translate a lot of them very easily. Due to all the various tubes, one of which was down his throat meant PJ couldn't and shouldn't try to talk.

Still feeling the shock of everything, Jean couldn't wait to find out what the HECK!, had caused this emergency condition. It was the worst feeling she had ever experienced. While all this was taking place, Jean hadn't realized until much later that her first blessing was being able to get there with no strains. She didn't even have to worry about the costs or how long to stay because she was now retired from working. Jean's health was also great so no challenges there and no spousal friction over spending their monies. With the way Jean rushed off with first getting the news they both knew that meant the possibility of many more trips to and from New York were very likely. Jean was standing right in front of PJ blessed that they could see touch and embrace each other. PJ's beautiful eyes were so focused on his mom, looking at her talking with his eyes "don't worry mom hold it together, I'm so glad you are here" was plain for Jean to interpret from his expressions. She had a flash back of when he was a youngster, how he never wanted his mommy to worry about anything. Coming into the hospital room she leaned in to kiss him again and again and when the tears started to fall they wet both their faces. Jean quickly turned her head to one side to conceal more of her tears flowing down her face. Why did she not want him to see her cry for him? Jean explains, she wanted him to see hope and faith and strength in her and not sorrow. Her whole head felt like it would explode any second from all the emotions she carried inside. She was determined to let smiles of hope out in front of PJ, instead she thought again of, the peace that surpasses all understandings, and wanted him to be able to rest with encouragement instead of fearing anything was wrong, he knew his mom had come to support and strengthen him. Jean was staying cognizant not to cover her eyes during any part of this challenge. She still felt numb yet frantic inside,......What?,...... How?,... When?,... just kept crowding her head as she stood at his bedside sharing long loving looks back and forth and holding his hand tight as he squeezed her hand back. Jean recalls even then his eyes were comforting her. PJ really knew his mom and could read her look of love, he knew his mom was aching to release the pain and tears. Everywhere on him were wires and tubes. After her stay in his room overnight and all the next day she could see PJ wanted all the tubes off, and he wanted to get up out of that bed to visit with his mom. The nurses had to gently tie his hands down to his side so he wouldn't intentionally pull the wires and tubes off. PJ wanted to be closer to his mom and not be restrained, he wanted to talk without tubes in his throat he wanted what he wanted. It was all so hard for Jean to know that her presence was causing a lot of problems. The third day PJ became very agitated and aggravated trying to talk around the tubes, moving his lips with no success which caused his blood pressure and other measured readings to elevate. It was as difficult for PJ to communicate as it was for Jean to witness, it was the helpless mommy syndrome, like when you have no control to make it better for your child. Jean talked with his team of doctors and was enlightened of many of the processes he was undergoing and how the medication was the contributing factor causing confusion for PJ. He physically looked in great shape, his weight was good, except his ankles were a little swollen and that too was the medications, Jean spent a lot of time rubbing his cold feet to invigorate circulation. Educated by his team of specialists doctors, Jean knew God had guided her to do the right thing from the start. She continued to just show a calm hope-filled face for PJ. While he laid in his bed of inserted tubes she noticed he didn't have on his glasses and her mommy instinct realized this would also make everything frustrating for him if he couldn't see clearly. Trying so very hard to stay strong, Jean kept saying in her head "It's all the test of Faith", just keep the Faith and stay calm for him! Jean realized that a lot more of her lesson was to just pray unending, …..this is when God and prayer are the only medicine.

Jean explained more about being in the hospital room, she would stand over his bed trying to imagine what PJ could possibly be trying to say to her with all the tubes down his throat. All the time Jean wanting to scream out loud in frustration for PJ, already realizing her presence was causing PJ to constantly be aggravated since he couldn't talk or anything and it was sounding off whistles on his monitoring systems. This meant his readings were changing, and that was not good. What's a mother to do?,… and right at that time she looked up and saw his extended family of New York all coming into the room to see him. Jean needed Rue because she felt all of her anxieties piling high. Wanting to collapse, scream and run out of the room was not the correct behavior either so Jean suppressed more of her feelings, also not good! Knowing that her sister and niece were out in the hospital family lounge, replenished Jean's fuel, and she thanked God for that. As any able-bodied mother would do, Jean kept standing there holding on to her son's hand to keep herself together. The visitors from his extended family came to see him, two Dominican women, both fluent in Spanish just like PJ including 80% of New York's population. When PJ saw them both his eyes gave Jean the reassurance she needed. Immediately they came up to Jean and called her mommie (strong Spanish accents) and they all embraced each other with tears flowing. Jean was more confused from this greeting because to Jean it seemed like they all had looks lacking hope. She didn't want that kind of spirit in the room. The way PJ was all hooked up, may have looked bad, but he had pneumonia which is known to be curable! Jean heard a lot about his close friends over the years. It would be the first time Jean would get the opportunity to meet Mercedes and the entire family. Right away both Mercedes and her sister extended the offer for Jean to come and stay with them during her stay in New York. They looked at Jean with same concerns as looking at PJ. Jean wondered if they had more to tell her but they didn't speak English. Jean just wanted to stay by PJ' s side and monitor his improvements. It wasn't long before Jean had bonded with all of PJ's friends, but she immediately knew she would need an interpreter for future encountering and this too was already provided. Jean's good friend (Mil) in Florida had been instrumental from the start in being her interpreter for the first calls about PJ's condition. She had been put in place over 27 years ago and now she made herself available to help. Mil was long distance with family and a job so Jean politely declined the offer to stay with PJ's extended family, indicating she would be by to visit really soon.

Jean had brought a focal point to sooth PJ as he lay there. She pinned it to his hospital room wall, it was a wonderful gift card from her sis-n-law. A spiritual greeting card in miniature box form and when opened it transformed into a beautiful cross. PJ's eyes expressed satisfaction just to see it. Jean could see the medications were taking effect and he was drifting in and out of sleep, so his New York family left saying they would be back. PJ smiled as his eyes were drooping to a close. Once PJ was fast to sleep, Jean rushed out to meet with her family in the waiting room. As Jean lifelessly walked down the halls, the pictures in the hallways reminded her of being in the hospital when her sister was ready to deliver her own son. Rue was in labor with her first child and all she wanted was for Jean to rub her feet to comfort her. Jean was soothed by picturing PJ pinning up a greeting card for his Aunt Rue's focal point. It was so loving, a Dalmatian mother dog with all her puppies and it was a tiny bit soothing for his Aunt Rue's labor pains. Jean said she now needed her sister in any comforting way possible. She wanted to let loose as loud as her lungs would allow her just to get some of the pain out. Jean realized it was time for her to pray again. She continued her walk down those white halls of a maze, while thanking God and asking him for continued blessings with PJ's health. God's blanket of courage and faith embraced Jean just as she approached the last corner to greet her family in the lounge. Jean wanted them to know how much she believed in God's power as she was being carried by him, like footprints in the sand! Hallelujah! God composed her once again. The family all embraced one another with swollen eyes while Jean was strengthened by God's grace. After the family sat in raw form all talking recapping the characteristics of PJ and seeing a few of the memorable snatched up pictures Jean had grabbed in hast to come to New York. Jean encouraged her family to go check in to their hotel. She knew her place was to stay right by PJ's bedside, she also needed to see some type of improvement before she could ever leave from it. She cuddled in a corner and cried.

Comfort for Jean came just to stare into PJ's handsome eyes, she never imagined a mute conversation could be so meaningful. Kisses all over his face and hands, keeping cool towels on his forehead, rubbing his feet, stroking his beautiful head of hair, talking with their eyes, were all simple treasures, unforgettable and priceless. A mother does all of these things when their children are born into the world as babies loving the nurturing concept, never imagining at the time of birth that it could all come back around again after they have grown into adults. Jean quotes, "Never take your blessings for granted, because each one of them (one-by-one) are even bigger than you ever imagined"

There are tons of PJ's joyous occasions, the memories of celebrating, performances, supporting and collaborating with family / friends to witness galore aspired achievements. Repetitively retracing all the accolades, it appears that PJ was on a personal mission confident to attain every one of his goals which he was blessed to do! At age 16, PJ worked for the

Children's Hospital in Ca as an Office Manager, one day Jean brought a plaque to PJ's office which demonstrated the clarity of everyone's individual success is painted differently. PJ loved it and he was quick to give his Mom aspiring gifts for her office. Jean stopped being shocked over the early achievements PJ acquired. His job titles definitely superseded his age. She told him often, to shoot for the moon because if he landed in the stars that was just as good. At that stage of PJ's life it was rewarding to see him using his vast array of talents, because it minimized and began covering up of the misdemeanor of being bullied. His new focus brought on continued accomplished successes for PJ. The signs that PJ was on a God Driven Mission from day one were undeniable. PJ knew what he wanted in a career and went after cooperate America like he had already attained a PHD in Business Management.

Looking at him now in the hospital bed sleeping soundly, Jean began to unfold his huge transformation since she last saw him. By the length of PJ's hair, her guess was that he had escaped at least two months without haircuts. It was like looking at a replica of Jesus lying there with his beautiful long wavy locks that touched his shoulders. Jean was placing cold towels on his forehead to help keep his temperature moderate, and was tempted to take pictures of him but she knew better not to disrupt the importance of their peaceful awarded time together. Phones and picture taking is a bad distraction which never deserves to be activated during intensive care. Jean smiles with gratitude that she followed her heart, focusing only on their time spent together. Being that she had already laid both of her parents to rest, she knew all about how a message from someone on their sick bed can be completely missed when distracted, and then later on you realize what the intended message meant. Jean agrees she unconsciously covered her eyes in that moment because everything was happening so fast and she just wanted PJ to recover and get back up on his feet, just as much as he wanted that for himself. No matter how much we re-track life's circumstances the more important lesson is to remember that it is already in the order intended. God has our names in his book of life with specific dates for our individual home going. Jean takes a long and silent, pause_ It was in that moment that Jean realized God had sent PJ into her life to help her grow and strengthen her posture for life's experiences.

She uttered to herself, "I trust God will do what is best in every situation." These were the types of spiritual foods that Jean fed herself just to ease her pain. The tears came down stronger than before, and that was okay, this was her cleansing. Jean still had her husband to lean on, thank God! Jean hung her head in heavy sadness, feeling selfish for so much that she had taken for granted such as thinking PJ would always be around for her. Just as Jean witnessed PJ's Dad and a lot of their family blood line be laid to rest, now it was PJ, her only child of 35 years, his time was called to be laid to rest. "Stand ye in the ways, and see...where is the good way...and walk therein and ye shall find rest for your souls." "Look to Me, and be saved, all you ends of the earth! For I am God, and there is no other" (Isaiah 45:22)

Back in New York, it's the night before Rue and family will head back to Ca. Jean decides to let PJ get some rest and she goes back to the hotel with Rue and family to share their room. She still felt strange leaving PJ's bedside but also knew he needed the rest. It was great to get a shower, eat something more filling and try to see if she could sleep. Of course that didn't work, Jean still felt compelled to hold back her awaited hard cry! Very early the next morning an amazing happening displayed in their hotel room. It was like the morning skies had opened up and these rays of light, 5 to be exact, were shinning down into their hotel room window. It was eerie, Rue was also awake to witnessed this. It only made Jean want to rush back to the hospital immediately, she didn't want it to have any significance whatsoever! So saying quick good byes, well wishes and thanks to her family, Jean hurried back to the hospital. Since her arrival to hospital, Jean had slept each night in PJ's hospital room next to his bed. PJ would awake every hour or two to see his mom right by his side. Even though PJ would always look so surprised to see her still there, he already predicted it was what his mom would do. This same particular morning rushing back in a cab to see that PJ was good, Jean also needed the chance to speak with his doctors who came around only very early morning hours. Thank God PJ was still recovering okay! The team of specialist all came to PJ's room and gave Jean a full report of his vital signs and test, in those early days it only meant that it could go either way, and time would tell. All of the team concluded with, it was so great that PJ was brought to the hospital in time. Jean was grateful too, but How, When, What happened,_ what caused all this?" This just has to have a good outcome. Jean's prayers were locked on PJ being back up on his feet. She wanted and needed answers. The doctors assured her they were doing everything possible and they anticipated good results in next couple of days. The doctors and staff were so caring and helpful for Jean, giving her such welcomed hope and it was all so comforting. To hear them say if all went well PJ would gradually get off the tubes, but it would still require that he stay in the hospital for observation once the tubes were removed. Jean wanted so badly to exhale but chose to keep praying instead. She knew she wasn't going anywhere for a while, she felt a little better because of the doctors report and loved all the daily attention and care PJ was getting. Jean's family insisted on reserving a room for her to return and spend another night in private at their hotel. Jean felt blessed to be able to stay in New York with no financial worries until she witnessed real recovery. More insight of God at work was the fact that our close family member Jaynae who grew up with Rue, has a daughter attending N. Y. State college who, unknowingly, lived directly across the street from PJ for years. Wow, they also were offering Jean a stay at her place if needed to extend. God's works are Amazing!

PJ was fluent in Spanish from the age of 15. It is one of many reasons why Jean supported PJ's decision to relocate when he turned 23. Here we all are, standing in a hospital room by PJ's bed side. Jean knew for sure she wasn't leaving his bedside to stay with anyone. She thanked God again for being in a religious hospital, she prayed there would be more of God's favor in works. The doctors were all quick to acknowledged when speaking with them that God is the number one Physician. The accommodations for critical patient family members were comfortable enough so you could stay right there in the hospital. Jean prayed without ceasing for both important men in her life. Her sick husband in Ca was showing signs of improvement, at least that's how he updated her, she hoped he wasn't just keeping her from more worry. Jean's heart was heavy and she wanted to see PJ up and able to breath on his own. When the time presented itself she would know but for now her focus had to be in New York.

"Peace I leave with you my peace I give unto you, let not your heart be troubled, neither let it be afraid" (John. 14:27)

"Yet a little while, and the world seeth me no more; but ye see me; because I live, ye shall live also". (John 14:19)

When PJ had shortly relocated to New York, he called to tell his mom all about how he made a real friendship Relationship with a Dominican lady name Mercedes. When he was hired by Micro Soft of New York, a Florida friend recommended PJ rent a room from a very good friend's home so he did. A few years later, with the success of his new job, he moved into his own apartment in the Bronx for about 3 years. All the shootings in the Bronx neighborhoods seem to be a regular scene and when PJ decided to finally tell his mom about them he'd already made preparations to move back to Manhattan with Mercedes who wholeheartedly welcomed him back. Jean revisits how PJ had gotten upset with her during one of her visits to New York because, she had got up early one morning and walked over to the open produce market without him. She had no idea that it was that dangerous in a seemingly pleasant neighborhood. Jean didn't know but when she returned to the apartment PJ was happy to see her and frantic about the possibilities. He then told her the real deal of Bronx lifestyle. It had Jean shaking in her boots, she really wanted him to come back to Ca. Crime was continuously climbing daily in the Bronx and PJ was then describing a scene in detail to Jean right outside their bedroom window of serious gun fire. Jean was ecstatic but so grateful that Mercedes and family had welcomed PJ back to Manhattan into her home. Jean couldn't wait for him to relocate. These remaining years rekindled PJ's Relationship with Mercedes and her family, they were a bonded family. Jean was at peace to know the Jewish Dominican family that PJ always talked about. This family amazingly resembled his Dad's family line, PJ described them to Jean as great people with no drama. Grateful! Mercedes has a son, a replica of PJ at age 9 and an adorable daughter age 2. Jean heard many a story about PJ's discipline techniques for the son, who grew up to appreciate PJ's love.

Jean realized all her single parenting struggles, had all been witnessed by PJ and he was inspired to be her little man of the house. She thought about all the disciplinary concepts she afforded him and noticed that he was reinventing that wheel for the New York childcare in their house. She knew PJ never wanted to have any kids and that had a lot to do with what his child exposure experiences had been. It was all such a mental heavy weight for a growing boy to carry all his early deceased family members; gifted with a high IQ rating; bullied endlessly by all; not having a father figure example during these times; wanting relationships with his half sisters; and much much more. Can you believe for most of the time, PJ still had the ability to reflect a positive and high spirited attitude. It was what empowered Jean to want to aspire to become powerfully successful for both their lives. Her enthusiasm to become all she could be for her son was her God given purpose in life. If it had not been for PJ's arrival, Jean admits, she doesn't know what her life would have been like. Her momma Mae prided in pleasing her own mother just as Jean wanted nothing more than to please her own mom. As a parent Jean wanted to learn from her mom all about sustaining strength and Marriage for the long haul. She witnessed their mother's life with all it's stressful demands and how skillfully she overcame every challenge. Jean and her siblings experienced most of life's lessons up close and personal right at home. There were times when Jean and her sister thought they could fight off their mom's small battles for her. momma Mae, stepped up to show all her children that the consistency of devoted Bible study resulted in unmovable faith and commitment to God's word. She repeatedly assured her children it was all she needed for her protection.

Jean was so happy to have such an intelligent minded young man with such insight. She could see that all the hater treatment had fueled her son to be all he could possibly be. While living in Ca he has accomplished so much for his age. Now PJ stayed on the internet checking out all the possibilities for relocating to pursue his dream job. He planned it all out to travel first to Florida, find temporary work while waiting for his opening spot at Micro Soft of New York. What confidence, he was on a mission! Jean reflects on every desire PJ pursued he was granted. Jean just shakes her head in astonishment saying that PJ was amazing to witness and when he spoke it was just enlightening. Jean only needed to pray for God's favor to keep him safe in is travels. Fearless, motivated and determined to explore new possibilities, that was PJ, impelled to get started on the first phase of his plan. Jean was excited for him too but nervous that he was going alone.

"I will instruct thee and teach thee in the way which thou shalt go: I will guide thee with mine eye." (Psalm 32:8)

She realized, wait a minute! Jean uncovered her eyes again, all of PJ's life God's protection had been over him. She knew she had to be strong, trust God, and continue to support, love and encourage PJ.

What did bring Jean to tears was putting all those thousands of miles between PJ and family. It saddened Jean. She instead gave him a personable send off with a few neighborhood friends. PJ was ready to go. With the many Christian warriors, family and friends all praying plus the gifts for traveling grace was all that there was time for. PJ was ready to go, and by the glorious grace of God, PJ made it to Florida safely. Jean stops hard and realized, this was necessary, because PJ was detaching from mom's apron strings for his mom to grow in strength which required distance. PJ use to comment on how much his mom needed and depended on him around the house. This is why PJ was so happy for Jean when she decided to relocate and marry. He was free to be his own man now. Once he arrived in Florida in time for the job fare, using his bi-lingual abilities, he was hired on the spot to start work for the luxurious Fort Lauder dale Resort right on Florida's beach front.

"My God shall supply all your needs according to his riches in glory by Christ Jesus". (Philip 4:19)

A job fair that a friend told him to check out, and after long waiting line he was interviewed and selected for job that same day. Jean told him he had to find a church home, PJ knew his mom would insist for it was required by God. PJ listened and was glad he did, there were times he needed a church to pray with him through his adjustments. The day came when he called his mom at work all excited! PJ received the call from Microsoft of New York they informed him he would be relocated to New York all paid expenses to start his dream job! Jean was ready to jump through the phone. She wanted to drop everything to be able to celebrate with him, he always accomplish his goals. Jean says, there are a lot of situation she could express to me about PJ's God given abilities that amazes everyone she tells. It was as though he had a connection and knew he would be granted certain blessings and he was off and running to full fill his dreams. Jean was tremendously blessed to be his mother. "My grace is sufficient for thee: for my strength is made perfect in weakness." (2Corith.12:9)

When PJ turned 22 he was determined to find his own place in life while still living in CA. He had experienced moving out on his own several times, with room mate(s), more than once. It all made PJ realize Ca was expensive but the opportunities were seemingly scarce, to PJ due to his then feelings that college was not a requirement for him to succeed. He had his own mind and wouldn't listen about college because so many had told him he was going to be successful no matter what. It was kind of like PJ knew something greater was his life plan and he was on a determined mission. Right after the summer at Qualcom Corp. in Ca, his dream job was Micro Soft of New York as an Office Manager. His resume was so incredible for his age, his saying at a young age was that to be a man was to get out on your own. PJ was excited to merely have accomplished being out on his own. Jean always felt that she would never stand in the way of his dreams, especially seeing how well he prepared himself. All of this talk with PJ making changes, motivated Jean to make changes she had longed to do. Retrieving her thoughts, she sees why PJ became so excited for her to make a move, he told his mom he had been hoping she would move and/or marry, so he could feel good about pursuing his own dreams. Now they were both inspired. Jean explained how PJ had always been the man for his mom and she could now see the weight lifted from him to go and grow. PJ had always kept hope as Jean occasionally struggled with single parenting, that a better life was coming one day for his mom and he felt the time was finally here. His assurance for both of their blessings was very convincing and they prayed together for God to continue blessing their entire family. PJ had faith that their move would motivate the masses within their Relationships to all make positive changes for their lives. It did inspired a lot of their family members which for some, gave new substance for their lives. New jobs, homes, cars, start of new businesses, etc...... it can sometimes just take one person to start a chain reaction of results. All the glory goes to God who truly makes it all possible.

CHAPTER 3

REVEAL (In PJ's own words, selected pages from his personal Journal!

<u>Relationships!</u> It is what begins the minute we are born and connects to the masses. We all began in this world without Choice! We come with God's placement. I have learned through all my studies and my travels in life that God granted me well. However, I do forgive my mother and father for making a child and not making a life together for me to grow up in! From the very beginning the Relationship is bonding with a mother as soon as we hit the air. From then on the inescapable multitude of Relationships evolves. I had to first grow up and renew daily the understanding of life's hand outs. My parents were just products of their own environment just as we all are. My mom sacrificed and gave me all she knew to give, influenced, of course, by her own experiences. I vaguely remember the pleasures of being around both parents at the same time but from all the photos my mom kept to show me later in my life, helped tremendously. I knew my Dad and Mom were married by all the memorable pictures so I was legitimate, but growing up, I didn't understand all the rest of it. I had questions. I assumed there must be pertinent reasons why my mom chose to talk very little about my Dad. Whenever she did it was always pleasant, without anger and I appreciated that but, I knew it had to be more to the story. Undeniably, it still left me puzzled. By the time I was approaching middle school, I, like so many deprived young boys to men, I really needed that Father son Relationship. My adolescent years were

very impressionable with more of my influence coming from five caring Relationships, my mom, my two Grandmas, 1 Great Aunt and my Aunt Rue (mom's Sister). The remarkable influences of five women in my life that sincerely had my best interest at heart was appreciated. So much love was there, and when I came outside of those protective walls, I witnessed so much evils. As a young boy this is where you need the guidance from a father figure. Somewhat blurred I can still recall harboring anticipation to fly on airplanes and visit with my dad, my little sisters and see my Hawaiian Grandma 'J'. I'd wished those Relationships could have stayed in my life. My Relationship circle was building I was also learning about classmates and their Relationship circumstances and the raw truth left me very grateful that I had a Relationship with my own dad. People should never let opportunities pass them by and not show love to who made their lives possible,... no matter what the circumstances! Hearing what some of my class mates dealt with let me know I wasn't the only one wanting parts of my life to be different! Those visits to see my dad shed crazy light as an adult now, I'm rewinding back and I can see why my mom and dad hadn't stayed married. I was young in age but I know what I witnessed. I saw a lot of things for myself, but I was careful not to spoil my chances to visit my dad again and especially to see my little sisters. I learned very early to keep all the dreary details of my visits to myself, which wasn't hard to do because my mom didn't really question my visits. I just recall her concerns were always about me and just being so glad I'd made it back safely. Mom may have wanted to ask but her concern was more about us getting back on track with our lives together. My mom was happy to have her little man back. The pictures revealed it all, I could see she seemed to entail every little thing like she was ensuring the truth to my story. I am glad and it was what I needed and more. I had strong love for family from the start. It brought to mind how I also wanted my little sisters to have some of my family love. My dad asking me to take them back home with me, he would tell me, "take your sisters, they would enjoy and benefit from your mom's love! I knew something wasn't right in their environment, but having the opportunity of seeing my little sisters and my dad was key for me. One of my return trips back to Ca, I asked my mom if my little sisters could come back with me for a visit, and my dad wanted it too. Dad would tell me how great my mom was and how much he still loved her and at my age, I was confused. My mom's answer was, it had to be okay with their mom, and it never happened. As a young confused boy, I kept dad's revealed life style to myself. Mom believed in God's protection and the importance of family ties for me. Because my mom maintained a great Relationship with Grandma J, she knew I would spend a better part of my visit with Grandma.

My mom was still loved as Grandma J's daughter, their Relationship was very close, you would have thought my mom and dad were still together! A Relationship I highlight. Check it out, both of my Grandmas became best friends when both my Grandpas were stationed together in the Navy. Therefor both my parents felt their reunion was a match destined to be especially for that reason. From all the pics mom, dad and I had a great beginning_ they stayed married 5 years, separated and then Divorced. As the years added clarity to my memory I revisited some of those scenes at dad's place. I also awoke to why I covered up some of those memories. I was 9 then and had brighter vision about the choices my dad made in the Relationships he maintained. Where they lived wasn't a great choice for children, the front door faced a very busy street in the heart of the city. My dad and lady friend both chose not to work. Dad and all of the flow of traffic in and out were all about drinking alcohol, smoking strange stuff and marijuana. There were things I noticed out the corner of my eyes, and unquestionably, very puzzling. I did know when to ask if my sisters and I could go to Grandma J's. I knew to keep this to myself and not tell mom, Auntie or my Grandmas. Most of my visits to dad's place reminded me of being somewhere you knew you shouldn't be. My sisters and I were always excited to go to Grandma J's, because those were the greatest memories for all of us. Grandma J's Hawaiian cooking, the games we'd play, it felt so good for me to see my sisters happy. There were good times with my dad being hilarious with jokes but those times were short lived. I was comfortably a more relaxed and enjoyable atmosphere at Grandma J's. Tension would easily flair at dad's place all associated with their choice life style. Whenever I left my sisters to return home it ripped my big brother feelings in half. I always wanted to go back home to the love my mom had waiting for me and the comforts of home but I never wanted to leave my sisters. The Relationship with my little sister's at dad's place is another book by itself. I desperately wanted to keep our Relationship connected but I somehow knew this would come to an end. It was amazing how my mom could give me hope about my sisters and our future, without even knowing all the secrets to the life style they had to live. Now that I look back, I guess my mom could imagine their life, she was married to my dad for over 5 years. I held on to her encouraging words, it helped me remove some of my worries, they did have their own mom. To this day I have never revealed any of those impermissible situations to anyone. At age 10, I had a much larger circle of Relationships, some I didn't need but many I greatly appreciated. Whatever type of environment children are raised up in can either make or break them. When children are blessed to have great surroundings and ample love plus spiritual balance it is something to appreciate. I needed God's help with the attempts I made trying to give my sisters the shield and armor to always carry. I always went home praying for their provided protection hoping to shield them from the devious atmosphere. Many times my dad would be incoherent and blind to all the possible fatalities around that place. His lady friend would be more attentive to all the traffic and her choices weren't wise either. Good home structure will provide spiritual balance with morale ethics and setting good examples help the implant. When the array of challenges strike, without structure the results are inevitable mental scaring. One day I will tell my mom all about dad's place.

I closed my eyes to recap one of my brighter memories,….. I'm sitting in the back seat of my Mom's car watching both my parents having conversations while riding near downtown. We stopped to park along a tall and wide chain length fence to watch the air Planes land and take off, a favorite pass time. This was how they prepared me for the way I would soon be going to visit dad and Grandma J! With emotional tones, mom would give me inspirations saying I could grow up and become a pilot if I chose to. That was a happy feeling, she wanted me to dream big. At my young age I recall wanting that car ride to last forever. I Do remember, I had witness the two of them laughing and singing together. That's a memory I hold close. Watching through the eyes of a child makes life seem so magnetized. Then when you recall the same memories as an adult it's modified. It is a lesson because now you are capable to make the difference for change in your own life by being an adult. It's taken some hard life lessons for me to learn why we all think different and want different things out of life. I had to find out what I wanted for myself, by myself, for my life and I knew I was being spiritual guided to do this on my own. Fearless!

It was great to have pictures, I could see my dad was happily in my life from my beginning and this also included my dad's first daughter. Before I was ever born my mom and my then 3 year old, older sister had shared in a lot of special time together. It was great to see my mom's fragrance portraying who she was then caring for dad's kid always with love. On occasion, at home alone, I took the opportunity to pull out the photo albums and take long looks for myself. Night College or Marketing Network meetings had my mom's attention and I was old enough to have 3 or 4 hours to spend leafing through all the pages and boxes of pictures. I saw my parents wedding, mom's pregnancy with my older sister all over her, Grandma J and the huge cast of family members, plus all the social time my parents had at parties and concerts, etc. I saw so many pictures of me with both sides of the family, I was a chubby baby. This all held great value to see who I was a part of, it gave me substance. When you are as young as 10 and don't remember all the specifics of your toddler time you do need a jump start to remember those times. These are the reasons a young child is preoccupied when he walks into a crowd of other children and get misunderstood. I had a lot going on during these years, the concerns for my little sisters, all my school curriculum, music, theater and to keep mom happy, I consumed discipline tactics through accomplishments in martial arts and baseball. These venues gave me better Relationship opportunities, my focus in school had shifted and the bullies I encountered were trivial to me now. I can't believe I had told myself I didn't want to be smart anymore due to that treatment. Funny! I was around people with mind sets similar to mind. I started applying my interest more in performing arts and music. I had dealt with so much mistreatment all through school and with some family from being knowledgeable. Mom even volunteered once a week to be a face on campus during my middle and high school years hoping it would help me out. I needed to grow up fast. I needed to be a man (no male role model) to carry all the weight. I earnestly longed to be accepted for just being myself. All males except one uncle in my family seem to be really struggling with that. It was always easier for me to collect female friends vice male friends which I attributed to my surroundings, most of my influences came from females.

I was raised in a middle class community near the bay and beach. It was predominately 90% Caucasian persuasion. My mom always gave me the talks of caution to steer me from any possible trouble because she said for me to be African American male would classify me as guilty no matter what the situation. Being young and green to all the racism, I didn't want to believe it. Where we moved from was a melting pot of ethnicity and she never felt the need before to give me this type insight or maybe it was just the time to tell me. Once we relocated to a house near the beach, our next door neighbors were seemingly good people. Their daughter Ellie, was my age and we hit it off instantly, we spent a lot of time together especially during summer months. Our parents were friends from as far back as when my Great Aunt lived there. Ellie and I did a lot; bike riding all over the beach, skating, watching the boat races at the bay and swimming at the Plunge. In our adventures we discovered beautiful Resorts close to the beach that had great private swimming pools so we decided we would come back and venture into these unauthorized upscale areas to enjoy great swimming vice going to the big over crowded Plunges. Ellie was my second stab at sex. We had big fun swimming at these Resorts, but in the back of my mind, I remembered what my Mom warned me about and how it could come true. I never told my mom about this either and just glad we never got caught. However, I did get the opportunity to experience mom's warning while living near the beach. There was a boy on our block who lived with his dad and was a real loner. His name was Carl and he wanted to hang out with Ellie and I, so we became a trio that particular summer. Ellie said she felt sorry for him, because it was evident that he had issues. Carl told us how good it was to finally have some friends and hoped we would remain his friends. That should have been a loud warning sign for Ellie and I but due to all the Relationship bullying that I had experienced, I didn't want to be quick to judge. Ellie and I both recognized his mood swings and temperament. Once high school started back we noticed that Carl wasn't going to school at all and when we asked him about it, he just said his dad let him make his own choices. Ellie and I knew things weren't right with Carl and we saw how rebellious he was with his dad. I was almost ready to pull away from the trio situation when it all became clear.

This particular day after coming home from school, Carl caught up with Ellie and I, he wanted to show us something. So we reluctantly followed

Carl about 1 ½ blocks away from our street. He told us how excited he was to show us this great place, it turned out to be an unattended house on a corner lot facing the main street. Once we got there we were puzzled as hell, what's up? Carl quickly ran around to the back of the house and came out through the front door calling for us to come in. Ellie, being the curious female, moved up to the front porch and peered inside asking him did he know who owned the property? I remember feeling like it was all a set up and how I would surely be the guilty one if anything went wrong! Thanks to mom's talk, I chose to stay back outside the fence. Carl kept at me to come in and I told him, I was going back home. He always seemed to have a bad streak in him and it was really showing now. Shortly after starting down the block telling myself he was up to no good, I could hear Ellie yelling for Carl to stop and calling him crazy! I turned to see her still on the porch flapping her arms at the door then covering her face. Still looking in their direction I could hear very loud crashing sounds coming from that house! Carl was literally destroying the interior of that house, like a mad man he was pulling down cabinets, kicking holes in the walls and ripping down curtains and more. He had wanted us to join in on that!? No way! I went back to insist Ellie get off the steps so we could get home. It was crazy to witness, Carl had gone berserk, a real basket case. You could tell he was releasing dark imbedded stuff like demons were hold of him. As we were walking back to our block, we could hear the noises had not stopped so we took off running to get home to tell our moms. My mom hadn't got home yet, but later that evening we got the loud hard knock at our door and I knew it would be the Police. I kept thinking about how I had seen the warning signs just hanging out with this guy, but I still wasn't ready for what we witnessed that day. I was about 13 then and mom had no need to be concerned with me being in any trouble and never with the Police. When she saw the Police Officer at the door she remained very calm and when he asked did she have a son named PJ, she nodded and invited him in. Mom called out for me to join them and the Officer began by saying Carl was a documented problem for this neighborhood for years and how they'd been called numerous times concerning him. He also added that Carl's father could not control him through all the years prior. They did everything to get Carl to attend school and he flat out refused. I was relieved the conversation started this way. Then the Officer said Carl had identified me, to be the one who destroyed the house and I was livid, in my head my Mom's analysis of what happens when crime is committed was happening right before my eyes, plain to see. I got so scared because I felt like it could really go bad for me because I was there. Once again I was let down by another so called friend, but this time a crazy person calling himself a friend! Relationships! The Officer also said he still had to talk with Ellie who was another named suspect, but first he wanted to get my statement of what happened. I was sure fire ready to tell him exactly what happened. At least I could include that I stayed outside the fence the entire time. Mom was right! It was a lesson I needed to learn for myself. The Officer almost assured us that he knew Carl was guilty. There were a few African Americans in the neighborhood radius of 5 miles, but you could count us all on one hand. The rest is history, Ellie gave her statement and we were cleared and Carl was charged. Shortly afterward, Carl and his Father moved out of the neighborhood and life was sweet again. In today's world that could have gone really bad, I was glad that I was spared. Relationships, I could see becoming a man was being very selective with your choices. It woke me up to understanding the logic to first observe and absorb a lot about people before deciding anything. My precious mom was always thinking I needed a man's guidance but she really wasn't doing a bad job at all. I had three guy friends who remained genuine throughout my adolescence and adult life. There were only a few of my Relationships to date that let into my personal feelings. I had a couple of girlfriends who I let become my venting towels, ladies just had great listening skills. My mind, intellect and appearance gave off maturity and it always attracted older ladies. These type Relationships were complicated and very challenging for a young man. I remember having empathy for two in particular who were already pregnant, jilted by their baby Dads, yet they were great people of character and while all the on-lookers judged them I chose not to. One of my lady friends had a Mom that didn't even want her. It was all hard to believe for me.

People usually don't know what a person carries on the inside and will judge your outward nature with their own synopsis, and mark you a candidate for bullying. Mom helped me to finally see that they themselves are also victims of bullying within their own environment. It still made my growing pains intolerable at times. I'm convinced now that it all must have impelled my (single parent) Mom to look to Jesus for all her strength to help me through my peer pressures. Mom's new found commitment aside from me and Grandma Mae, was serving in the Church. They both worked and served hard like they were paying off a never ending debt. The enhancement from their labors afforded me the best tools to circumvent my daily challenges. All in all, it intrigued my own curiosity to educate myself in-depth with God's word. As I began to implant myself into this study, it provided me the repellent and insight to pull out all my strengths to get through my peer pressures.

As my babysitter, my grandma Mae showed me her world of community outreach. I was the second grandchild but the first to get this type experience with her then involvement working for the Mayor of our city. Soon after my privileged opportunities it was a need for many of my cousins to come to Grandma Mae's. All of the children stories, songs, games as well as her community services had all been my introduction to a business administrative world. I really loved it.

My Mom over compensated trying to fill the void of lacking a Father figure. She prayed it wouldn't short change me so she exposed me to her world starting with her Government job on the Naval Base. Her high position afforded me the opportunity to board the many different Aircraft Carriers, visit the actual Helicopter hangers, board several different types of Air Planes, Helicopters and I was allowed to walk through the Logistics Admin offices where it was fully automated systems that caught my immediate attentions. I was intrigued that this was all under my mom's management during her regular work day. She was the head Boss Lady over all these departments and her staff consisted of both military and civilian personnel. They had great respect for her or just wanted to make points, either way, they showed me some great things about the Naval Base and it all inspired me to want to have a great job. I was proud of my mom's work position, I saw how important of a role she had but what stuck with me was what she had gone through to get where she was. On occasion she took me to night College with her, she even exposed me a little to her entrepreneurship in marketing. I get full now, remembering the ambitions my Mom worked to implant in me. She also encouraged me to get more involved with the Church youth programs, but my Mom and Grandma didn't have a clue that all it meant to me was more antagonizing bullying patterns from the youth would be added to my life. Instead I just acted as though I wasn't interested in those programs. I saw how my mom was blind to the reality of how I was being treated and more focused on how much I had to offer knowing the Bible the way I did. I knew I had the ability to give sermons because I wanted to tell the bullies so much and I chose not to. To stand in front of all those haters was nothing I wanted to subject myself to. I remember this was what started the typical teenage breakdown in communication between Mom and I.

The thought of re-marrying to help with my trying teen year was out of the question for Mom. She compensated by securing me with a heavy curriculum to keep me grounded and busy. By the time I was 9-10 years old, my dad had admitted his failures to me even though by then I had interpreted the reasons that caused their Divorce. I was growing up fast but still I had a lot to learn. I was being miss-informed by certain family siblings how they wanted to falsify our family ties. If only I had just gone and asked mom myself, but back then, I chose to wait until later. I could already see that my mom was hard on the men who wanted to or did date her, and because of that, I felt she was still carrying some pain from being married to dad. Mom wrapped her whole world around me and she was in no hurry to have a romantic Relationship with anyone. I remember it well, she had the beauty to turn heads where ever we went and many times I purposely acted up just to redirect guys attention from my mom. While I was in 4th thru 6th grad, mom just wasn't interested and I knew her focus was really on all my curriculum.

Something I will never forget was one particular day, my mom came to pick me up after work and Grandma Mae flat out told her "You need to get a life, and make some room for new friends, don't put every single moment of your free time into your son,". Grandma let mom know that she would be her babysitter even after hours, Grandma was the best! She even told her "Go get yourself pregnant and have another baby"! I remember that conversation because I thought how great it would be to have a little brother or sister right there at home with us. But mom sucked her teeth and said 'Oh No, not without marriage'! I know it affected my mom because later she asked me if I would like for her to have another baby. I knew how full mom's hand were and all her efforts to make us a good life, I wanted to tell her yes but I also wanted her to be rescued from all her struggles. All through my elementary school days, on up to my teens, I remember how much my mom spoiled me. I loved seeing her coming to get me after her work, she was always bringing me surprises, taking me places, but now she needed to have some fun of her own, new friends could lead to a lot. I was comforted knowing I always had Grandma in her absence. In the beginning, I had great friends in Grandma's neighborhood. Grandma was wise, polished and admired by all in her community I was well educated going to all those places with her and then it all came a screeching halt, the new day came when a few of my cousins also needed Grandma's baby sitting time and attention. A lot changed then because I had to share Grandma and the boy cousins were there to move me completely out. My circle of neighborhood friends had also become influenced by my male cousins, turning my fake friends around to teasing the naive PJ. On the flip side, one of my girl cousins was wanting/needing too many hugs and kisses from me. All I knew then was that they were a few representations of my family members. Teased enough about being a crybaby and snitch, I didn't tell mom about any of it. I had a mountain of strange and weird things coming at me, a real uncomfortable feeling. I knew I needed to hurry and grow up so I could sort out the massive confusion of Relationships in my life, crazy! Can't wait to make my own choices. Grandpa's presence didn't help much at all, he never made me feel like he had my best interest at heart, he took sides during confrontations with cousins and it would never be in my favor. Oh Yeah, I wanted to hurry to grow up to make my own choices and be in different environment. I always looked forward to my seeing my mom but I knew I needed male role model.

When it was just me I use to go everywhere with my Grandma, but now with all the cousins and myself we all stayed back with Grandpa. Notice, I never brought him up as a male role model. Grandpa found it easier to go and drink out of a brown bag covering his alcohol bottle which he kept in his bedroom or in the garage. His grandchildren fell in second place to his private drinking. It made me wonder if growing into a man was much more challenging than for women. My dad was heavy into drugs, both Grandpas were closet drinkers, several uncles on both sides of my family were dead due to drugs,... what's up with this? When it came to our Grandmas we all (seemingly) found it compulsory to give and show automatic love and respect over the Grandpas. Relationships! I had a Great Aunt who lived by the beach, she was always telling me Bible passages and scriptures to learn. Then she'd quiz me each time I saw her. Her spiritual guidance started when I was very young. Mom explained to me after leaving dad how we went and stayed with Aunt Nie. It was a great spiritual place for mom to cry a lot and recover. My great Aunt was a happy widower who did everything to help everybody. She was the one who told me I was given special favor from God. I remember this Aunt being so encouraging for me, she would say I am going to grow up to be greatly admired and loved. I think she was easing my bullying pains. Yes Aunt Nie was also a strong Christian woman. Her house was full of plants and mirrors, a regular place that we went to visit many times after we got our own place to live. I liked playing with her white cat, 'Snowball'. Sometimes we would surprise visit her Church and take Aunt Nie out to eat after wards because my mom didn't care for cats and just wanted see Aunt Nie.

It didn't take long for me to connect with all the prayers of favor directed at me, I paired it up with a keen sense of logic and I could strangely feel what God had afforded me. My level of confidence spiked as I plugged into the realization of being truly gifted. I needed to implement my gifts in the time given me. I somehow knew what made my learning skills so natural, school aptitude tests and any test were easy. The more I matured, my intellect caused me to be outcast by my peers.

Being smart in class was frowned upon, at least they didn't want it coming from me. I knew it affected my disposition…. but I woke up and realized all the haters were not going to be in my world all of my life.

By the time I reached a qualified age to work, my high school counselor assigned me to a program that allowed me the space to work part time requiring that I sustain good grades. This counselor told mom she wished more of the students had my mind set. My scores easily qualified me, the counselor commended my attitude for business. My ability to succeed with this school/work program had me excited. This opened up a whole new world and circle of Relationships for me. I started working, making my own money and I knew what I wanted in life. I had a strong desire to work for cooperate America. Rejuvenated and on my new course of life, I was excited about the summer hire program for students. This is when it all clicked in my head that I would receive much of what I aspired to attain. I even recall waking up some mornings visualizing future world news headlines concerning new ideas that people blocked to envision. It felt like I was still dreaming, I'd wake up flooded with the possibilities. Whenever I enlightened my ideas to people in my circle, of course they found me to be strange and unusual. At the end of my days, the reward came to be by way of female influences. They were the great listeners who at least were fascinated to hear me talk. It caused me to keep opening up to the understanding of my position of favor. Feeling so connected to it's advantage, all I can say is, incredible rewards began to pour out. Always encouraged by my mom, I read a lot, including listening to her motivational business administration tapes. I played the piano, and introduced myself to writing poetry/songs, and mini Bible sermons, etc. I called it luck, but there were blessings falling out all around me. I owe my drive for success to my Grandmas, mom and two Aunts. They believed in me and contributed greatly to my successes. Their regular nurturing of love, patience and understanding were their investments in me. It cleared away a lot of the junk in my roads traveled and it's replacement was my swollen level of confidence. Love works, God is Love!

At age 18 to 21, still careful using my tool of choice I had attain many accolades still pushing forward. I knew I had to go see the world, I wanted to choose new scenery. I definitely wanted plan outside the box and not be complacent to stay in one place all my life. My new energies were locked on organizing my relocation. Confident it would all happen, my feelings were electric, it was time to soar even higher. My prayers remained with mom and women of influence would accept my choices. With anticipation and excitement, I imagined all the positive possibilities in store. The Relationship with mom taught me all about making choices, she herself learned early to let go and let God while supporting my needs. I always saw kids my age doing faddish stuff and mom knew I wasn't a follower. I eventually told her about my thirst for wholeness, I needed my own identity (name change) it help tremendously! I worked so I saved up my own monies to attain and pursue a legal name change. Completely standing by me, mom supported my decision to change. I realize that at the end of the day, she even knew all the details concerning my reasons why. I loved my dad but I no longer wanted the same name he carried. Single parenthood for mom was all about survival requirements and it blinded her a little from seeing the importance of being told my birth story. She felt as though she was sparing me by not bringing up those outrageous details on dad. She didn't know that I had a few of my own. The name change was what I needed because I had to carry around his exact same name, already contaminated name. The love of Grandma J and my new found heritage allowed me to plug into my roots in a different manner. Once I started working, my dad's name and his foul paper trail always crossed over to me and it was a hindrance. This was one of the mental scars dad left me to deal with while I was trying to develop as a man. A lot had transpired over the years with my sisters and their mom, but I was still requesting they come visits, but constraints would not allow it. Mom's words of wisdom were, the time will present itself and only when it is right, and my sister's will be able to make their own decisions for their lives.

When I meditate, I see many times where my mom would pacify each request I made. It was like a medicine for me, called hope. Finally at 28, I know a lot about my life story, things were kept from me until I was grown. Almost identical to mom's situation, she didn't know her story until she was about to turn 30. In comparison I was relieved that I at least knew my dad and I was fortunate to have shared in his love and time. Now I'm educated to know my story in it's entirety. I was born to a Father who died as a result of a three part heart attack, third one being massive, he was 41 years old. The evidence, not all revealed, stated it to be substance abuse, and I saw first hand, part of what caused it. Does a massive heart attack, leave blood stains all over the floor? I was born to a loving, overly protective, mother who chose to spare me from that life. I even witnessed what our lives could have been like from the visits with my little sisters. Knowing my mom's character and her up bringing, she would never have meshed with that life. My dad's indulgence of substance abuse was horrific. Now that I had the big picture and so much was now crystal clear, it was time for me to show mom I was molded with God's powerfulness so she would stop worrying. It was plain to see why she'd worn the camouflaged battle scares of the past choice to leave her marriage. Mom tried hard to conceal her anxieties, praying that I wouldn't grow up influenced by dad's life. A year before my dad passed away, we started to get a lot of really late phone calls, actually, it was early mornings during the weekday calls from dad and family. I recall hearing those familiar background noises reminding me of being at dad's place. I had to get up for school and my mom had very early working hours so she was not happy, those calls came in at 2 to 4 A. M. in the morning. It would be dad's lady friend wanting to plan Disney World trips for us all while sounding under the influence of some type of drugs or alcohol. I already knew their household and these type calls translated to mean it was about drug infested Relationships. I could hear all the commotion in the background and my only concerns were about my little sisters still being deprived of proper rest. I still hadn't told mom all those details and I had since stopped flying out to see them. Those phone calls were transparent to us both and mom didn't appreciate it, she calmly explained to me why it had to stop! No calls after 10:00 and I agreed, it was fair. I found out later through other family that my dad's lady friend was also caught up in that life too. My mom just prayed endlessly asking for God's favor to keep me protected. The devastation weighed on her now that she had let dad off the hook of paying any child support for me because it was taxing to singularly pay off all the outstanding bills. Bills that they made together and even his previous bills because he no longer had a job. This silent rage she carried deep within her during the early stages of their divorce, and she would let it out at times. Dad could no longer hold a job anywhere due to his addiction and when they first separated, my mom was the only one working.

Mom made the decision to divorce and still preferred it that way. Agreeing to free dad of his obligations for me. Mom knew he already had hell to pay for living his choice life style. My safety and protection meant more to her than a child support check. I still revisit the day mom asked me if I remembered a birthday gift from dad of a motorize motorcycle? Of course

I did, it was the only present I believe I ever got, but it was the best gift! It took a lot of Bible study, prayer and time but my mom slowly erased her frustrations and renewed her whole outlook and with God's love it changed her disposition even more. Mom was happy again! She felt no need to back track. She learned to moved on with her life. I've made sure to journal every thought or concern from young to current as to one day use it for my book, and I must admit, hearing dad's detailed story later in life was God's timing. To have learned this as a youngster would have destroyed me, for there was no room to add it to my existing upheaval. I look at my mom with even more love for her choices made,_ God is good, all the time, and all the time, God shows his goodness. I have observed and absorbed enough to see how blessed I've been as he continues to bless me. All mom's involvement as a single parent, was to give and teach me direction. She wanted to make up for my not having a father, and so careful to not bring any other craziness to our lives.

Now, I see with her eyes! She continued to build herself and our lives back together without lax, going back to college at night while working, getting all the necessary credentials which awarded her humungous promotional job opportunities, placing her with Captains and Commanders of the Naval Forces. All these and many more steps to expose me to the best she possibly could, but the ultimate was all her efforts of putting God at the head to aid me with all my walks in life.

I observed her solid friendships throughout her circle of Relationships and whenever any of the many house repairs came crashing down unannounced friends would be right there to bail us out. Her association with community outreach projects exposed her to all types of venues and it helped us to resolve otherwise astronomical conditions. All the upkeep and management was enough to make one person buckle but Mom knew how to get help at minimal costs by offering to do professional facials or complete hair make overs. Genius! She had a flair for making people feel special with home made lunch or dinners to say Thank You. Phenomenal to watch, that was how my mom got us through. Grandma and Aunt Nie taught her well. To journal is recommended to help people open their eyes, I can see how much mom provided for my life. While in my teenage fury,

I could have easily missed a conscious lesson. All that my mom did was creating a champion in me. My mid teen years, I infringed a rotten period but it rendered a tough skin at the right time for me to withstand much of the contaminates forth coming. The toughest lesson learned was to constantly keep and carry God's word as my shield. It took several bumps and knocks in the road, but when it finally resonated within me, it caused me to grow fearless. The determination to become successful with my new identity, was a refreshing look to the future. All those trials of bullying were where I used my gifts to stand and go in the opposite direction from the masses. Those early growing pains have all subsided. I was excited to take on many different career ideas passionate to me, I was ready for the world awaiting. No one can think there won't be setbacks, or that all things planned will fall in the order like you want it to.

Attending my dad's funeral with mom was yet another hard growing pain. From a male perspective, a young boy always needs a father, a male role mentor, to teach him all about life. Mom wanted this for me too, but she froze with skepticism after trying several methods of support, through family, church members, close friends and even the Big Brother Program, none of those, unfortunately, were the right choice. Mom explained to me the necessity to be very selective of who you leave your children with. There will always be evils in the world, every type relationship experience can show cause for skepticism, even within family. I chose not to tell mom about everyone of my experiences growing up, who does that?! When she would ask me certain personal questions I would tell her exactly what she wanted to hear. I repetitively heard her imbed in me, "Study your bible, go to school, get good grades, become bi-lingual, stay out of trouble and one day God will bless you abundantly with continued gifts"! She took me with her to 'Rescue Mission' downtown to perceive and feed the homeless. I saw so many people who were just down and out, it made me think of my dad and sisters, and I prayed this would not be the end result for them. I even prayed they would not despise me for having had a way out. When I was about 15, and had wormed through those defiant teens, mom and I took our communication skills to new heights, she'd even started sincerely asking my opinion about things. A break through! I had silently struggled thru more than I had let out. I loved that we had finally attained the ability to effectively communicate. The tables had really turned, she honestly wanted my input on so many different topics and she attentively began listening to my point of view. I recognized and appreciated it all, I was a teenager, my life experiences were rapidly occurring, and I had to figure them out for myself. I had physically transformed, gifted with inherited good looks and now the lady friends were approaching in a rainbow of choices. My mom noticed all the changes in me but she hadn't noticed I was sneaking her car once she went to bed. :) I had a lot of room to explore, praying that I never got caught without a driver's license. I think my Aunt Rue saw me one night, Close Call!

Grandma Mae coached mom to use reverse psychology on me, while giving me room to make my own decisions. This was a great concept, it had me thinking I had made the choice when it was originally my mom's idea. Mom no longer lectured me, instead she was always asking me how I felt or what my goals and needs were. Looking back, I can see how she awarded me the space to grow up,_ by stepping back when she felt it was appropriate, and letting me paved my own way.

Man! That had to be what is called tough Love! Her constant work ethic, in spite of my temperament, was keeping my head clear of negative input which came from every direction. She always called me handsome even when I was loaded with acne, she just made me feel good about myself. My Mom experienced her own level of bullying growing up and knew the day would arrive for my bullying experiences to cease. Even though it had been her practice to not spoon feed me, she incorporated several tough love concepts to make me stand up or give up. Sometimes that is the best way to raise a boy, the best results depends on how a growing child reacts to it. I can see how vital a woman's role is and why God made them. Without a woman's touch it would be a cold and cruel world.

My first choice for a lady friend Relationship was when I was finishing 10th grade and she was finishing 12th. She was fine and well groomed young lady, already college bound. I met her at the mall and invited her to my Church of choice, we had a great connection with so much in common. I brought Bryanah home to meet mom, and the two of them had immediate chemistry and in no time they were laughing and talking as though they already knew each other. From the mall we rode the bus to my house with promises I would get her home safely that evening. I quickly changed for our evening at the movies which mom gladly escorted us to. We arrived at the movies and I saw mom's wink of approval. This was the first significant feeling for me of a great beginning, she accepted and liked the person I was. A memorable Relationship, then she was off to college, it happened to fast, we both hated that this Relationship was so abruptly challenged by distance. She left an imprint on me that I knew I could not get back. She complimented me on my entire demeanor, I think if she had stayed in my life she would have had the power to redirect my entire journey. Our age difference was no threat either, but long distance Relationship only lasts a minute, and soon the letters and emails stopped. She was a very special and polished lady, yes a Lady! None could measure up after Bryanah, a great memory for life. It was so short lived that every time I mentioned her to others, I had to be making her up, People! I am so glad my mom had personally met her and knew what affects she had on me. Who cares what other people think! Much later down the road, I tried selecting a lady at my church, yes still older than me and very attracted to me. This experience wasn't a good match, she was very appealing but came with lots of drama and eventually revealed all her insecurity issues. She had her own car and apartment but our age difference caused a lot of complexities, I can't believe it lasted almost a year. Even when she came to the house to pick me up, mom never saw it as more than just the church choir circle of friends.

Did I feel the need for counseling after my dad died? That was the question asked after about 6 months of my silent suffering. I had peace from the assurance to know my dad was finally at peace, so I declined! I recognized my healing was already in place by the regular and continuous spiritual guidance I maintained. I saw firsthand that my dad was unhappy with a lot plus the drug trap of which he was finally set free. The spiritual shield and armor I tried to use and wear worked for me sometimes, I did have my times of private grieving. I kept up with my Bible study, and several other reads, such as T. D. Jakes, (Lessons for Men), 'Rich Dad, Poor Dad', 'I'm Okay, You're Okay', "Who Moved My Cheese" etc. Without notice, Grandma, mom and myself all found ourselves in spontaneous fellowship at mom's house several times. We would sit and talk about a lot of different topics, opening up about our own individual feelings. This is how as an adult I finally learned all about my mom's detained life story with Grandma there to confirm.

I found that it also Incredible how no one is alone no matter their circumstances, you must be strong to stand up to whatever is on your plate. I loved the feeling of being with Grandma and Mom they had no judgmental bones in their bodies, no need for airs or phony attitudes, just be yourself and the love is the same. helped me move thru my misfortunes. After seeing what many of my classmates were dealing with completely cured me of my so called misfortunes, their situations were unmentionable, Man! I wouldn't even know how to handle some of those situations, I humbled myself and we all prayed at Mom's kitchen table.

From 1999 to current times, all young adults who managed to survive, will be the new spiritless breed. I have to keep the reminder that we are all products of our environment. I lacked a dad, but I still had a lot to be thankful for and I was taught to thank God on a regular. My generation was caught up in a whirl spin of sufferings because one or both of our parents were doing drugs and or weren't taught how to be parents. Some young people I know literally have nothing even close to experiencing what love from family feels like. My development into manhood was happening while I witnessed a lot of cruelty but so glad it included the influential polished women in my life of whom I listened to. Due to this consumption, I know I wanted to be knowledgeable about life so I began to open up about a lot of my own experiences to get proper insight. I was the engine that empowered and fulfilled my mom's purpose and I wanted to be of great service too. I found that great purpose in befriending a young paraplegic boy in my school named Lucas. There was nothing corrupt about him and I felt the need to reach out and help him and I did. This service became just as rewarding for me and his parents loved me for volunteering to work with Lucas. I wanted to also make mom proud of me, when there was really no need to. My mere existence was guaranteed love for my Mom.

By now, it was much easier to ask Mom a few more details to my story. When I was well pass the age of 14 and trying hard to stay connected with my Dad's side of family, I learned of some false allegations concerning the order of dad's choice steps of life. They perceived my story to be their own version, which puzzled me leaving me to question their input. I was ready to get the uninterrupted facts from my mom. She had never expressed anything about their married life together, and right after asking her, I could see a change come over her. Her first words to me were that I listen with open mind and visualized it all looking through her eyes only. She started from the beginning of how they met all the way to his last days. I did expect emotions to rise in her but she handled it very well. Amazing that she still carried no hostilities, only a few tears. She told me her tears were of joy because I had spent time with my Dad. Mom was so glad she had not robbed me of that time by being angry. It was great to hear how I was born into existence. Confirmed! They were in love and I was the result, my story was like a movie! I was not the reason they separated, Mom just refused to compete with the drugs. She was naive and vulnerable which made it very easy for her to miss a lot of the signs that identify a drug user. The intricate details of all the horror it brought into our lives, could have concluded our lives where you would have read about it in the media headlines, family found in home, etc. The scene explained was mom recalling, one of dad's crazy customers came to our home insisting my dad was there and exposing the butt of his gun to my mom. In a state of rage this man felt he had been scammed of his money by Dad. I was a toddler and even though my mom was scared out of her head, she went into survival mode. Standing at the door holding me in her arms she asked the man to wait outside, while she call him on the phone_ By the time mom finished telling me all the details she was emotional and I was in awe. Mom knew why she had re-framed from telling me all this, and added, she could write a book! To me that meant there was still a whole lot more to the details and she chose to leave out. Dad was blessed to marry mom, his concealed track record was corrupt, I guess he hoped some one good, like my mom, could help change his life. The level of respect I reserved for my mom went through the roof. To conceive how she never entertained aggravated feelings about my dad for me to witness revealed how she replaced it all with the love they had me. I've always seen the love of God in my mom.

I was correct to have suspected the misappropriated information given me concerning the dad who fathered all his children. Now fully matured and in my adult mind, I sensed their need to fabricate my story and add substance to their own existence were the reasons why! I am refreshed to know and now have read the supporting facts disclosed in my dad's apologetic letters to my mom, (his unique penmanship), was so satisfying for me.

When I would visit dad's place, he would say things to me that had no meaning as a youngster, but later on as an adult I comprehend those conscious messages. He made it known to me that he had too many wrong choices and was always apologizing to me for not being able bodied to be a father. Each time I returned to visit, I witnessed the concentrated focus on his hustle for making money and his carousing condition. Mom, putting her arms around me, insisted that I not harbor any old feelings, she had saved her letters for my clarity at the right time. I didn't need mom to explain anymore I had all my questions answered, it was well covered. I thank mom after all the years, for allowing my unimpeded Relationship with him. I understood the timing for my dad's divine call home and I am grateful and appreciate God's plan. Was I glad that my mom never drilled me for any pertinent details about my visits at dad's place? Yes! Some of the strange Relationships at dad's place I chose long ago to forget. My mom put me on solo flights to another city from ages 6 to 10 all nerve racking for her, but her love for me prevailed. Writing these journals reminds me to see and over turn everything, the good, bad and the ugly for it upsets most families. My dad had two more daughters out of wedlock after he and mom divorced. Dad was about 34 when he rescued a young homeless woman, after he had resorted to living out of a Motor home. This very young lady saw my dad as her hero. He felt great to rescue both her and her mom from living out in the cold. Every man needs his strokes, and to be looked upon as a life saver lifted him high. Dad's life of choices had brought about serious change. He only owned what was in his inherited motor home so instead of working a real job, he chose to hustle the streets. As time passed it was a real struggle and the hustle wasn't enough. There were now new little mouths to feed, it got so bad that my dad followed his mom and took his new family to northern Ca where Grandma J had recently relocated. Dad's hopes and dreams were that he and his lady friend would have a fresh start. They'd hoped to get jobs and soon have their own place. As often as I visited my dad, I saw no future in that becoming a reality. Dad's drug addiction was the weight tying them all down. Dad's lady friend was all caught up in the their hustle and I could see things that mad it clear to me I wouldn't be allowed to keep coming on visits unless I was going straight to Grandma J's. The hustle got real serious at the Motel room where dad lived. It was a regular hangout place, people always stopping over, not caring that we kids saw a lot. It wasn't a fun place for kids, we wanted to go outdoors to play, but this meant walking out the front Motel entrance right onto the busy streets of traffic. My mom would have had a fit if she had known about the condition of my stay. Dad's girlfriend was too playful, like a kid herself, she had OK housekeeping skills, but the existing infiltration of bugs were everywhere. We'd cook all our meals in the electric skillet and I remember not being so happy about eating. I knew I'd have to inconspicuously ensure those bugs weren't flying back home with me. This is where I remember wanting to hurry to visit Grandma J's house, it was more like home. I was really proud to be a big brother and have the chance to grow up hanging with my sisters but there was big challenges to be there. I thought about how I could have missed out not having any chance to know my little sisters or see dad if my mom had just refused. There are a lot of angry single moms in the world who fight to keep their kids away from their dad's. Then they grow up, and it makes for huge inadequacies. My Relationships with my Grand parents in northern Ca were great. My Hawaiian Grandma J loved my mom and always told her not to worry when I went to visit. My half sisters and I knew that we would be together at Grandma J's house it was much better to go there than be at the Motel. Her great cooking, and clean house relaxed me and my sister's, we had big fun. We didn't want it to stop. This was the real comfort my mom had in letting me visit dad, plus I knew, I could get some real sleep at Grandma J's.

If Grandma J hadn't called all the relatives together during one of my visits, I would have never learned so much about my ancestral family tree. I was blessed with several ethnic cultures in my blood line. The trips to northern CA gave me the chance to meet so many of my relatives on Dad's side. My Dad was Hawaiian, Samoan, Filipino,

Spanish and Black. That experience energized and motivated me to learn Spanish, I had also been persuaded by my Mom for years. Now I speak fluent Spanish!

My Grandparents in southern Ca where politically involved with the community. I learned a lot from hanging out with Grandma Mae doing her volunteer Service for the Mayor, she headed up the 'I Love a Clean San Diego' campaign. Mom's family had close family ties, especially while my Grandma lived. The family bond was a great source while both Grandma's were living, lots of relatives, would all come around, showing up for beach parties, big house parties and other gatherings. Grandparents are sacred for family unity, and when they pass away that weakens the tradition. I've watched on both sides of my family, how it gradually and drastically disconnects family. The great family pictures of togetherness start to weaken. Mom tried hard to explain how it doesn't mean that love is gone, but I knew from my own experiences with family, so I accepted her explanation for now. I realized that Relationships were much stronger between the Grandparent and each family member vice amongst one another. I even hoped with the loss of my dad, more family members would be caring and considerate and pull closer together for my upsets. It doesn't feel good when you are attending a family wake or 'Celebration of Life' and the Reality unfolds. Hate, Jealousy, Envy, Resentment, etc. if we all could be a fly on the wall, not very pretty.

I could hear my mom always trying to give me the positives to look towards, I knew it was pacifying when she said she wished she could give me a brother or a sister but not out of wed lock! Mom just didn't see where she could be married and be able to have children in a short allotted period. She was in her late thirties approaching 40! She focused more on the here and now trying to fill my void, rounding up my male cousins and classmates to have sleep overs putting up tents in our back yard, taking my cousins and I on outings to cool restaurants, even sneaking pizza into the movies so we could have real food with our movie, always trying to make life fun for an only child. She'd conjured a premeditated plans for so many adventures, hiking, museums, plays, concerts in the park bringing a really big purse and surprises were always inside. She bring the neighbors kids or family and I was thrilled she had done it. My mom was teaching me all about sharing so I wouldn't think all things evolved around only me.

Then I'd go back into the world of bullying, I recall being a target for humiliation by some of my cousins, they didn't seem to care that I had no street knowledge instead they would use it against me. Where and how I was raised, left me clueless about 'Playing the Dozen's. I literally lost my mind, the minute they started laughing and making insults about my, mom and Grandma, remember I was arrogant when it came to the five influential females who gave me a reason to believe in myself. So I took this game to be serious. Not a shred of street life mentality in me. The guys were ready to cast me aside as a crybaby, they were more concerned to appear cool in front of each other than helping to educate my understanding. As we all grew up I then could look back and identify that each one of them were all with personal private disheartening challenges themselves, things that really hurt. The difference was they had brothers and or sisters to help get them through. I was a solo soldier who got shot down a lot. As not to have idle time, mom kept me with agenda, I went to church, school, baseball practice, swimming lessons, Theater Rehearsals, Boy Scouts, Karate, singing and piano lessons. Not all at once, but spaced out enough to equip me with Human Relations. That opened me to a lot of Relationships. It gave me the opportunity to meet more and different types of people. I met and formed some quality friendships in these venues. The more I learned about different people, the more I realized as adults we should all learn to be more considerate but it still had it's flaws. When I would discuss my frustrations at the close of a day with Mom, one of her favorite sayings used a lot was "Oh how I wish You could see with My eyes!" I would conceal a quiet laugh to myself, I wanted to tell my mom so bad, that there was a whole lot about life she hadn't seen with her eyes!

I distinctly remember one of those times she took me with her to night college, one class in particular was Psychology, her purpose in mind was to give me more insight about making life choices plus allow me to see a mentor type exploiting my potential of what I could become. I remember the African American Professor (Mr. B) very conservative but poised, and surprised and impressed that I had come to college with Mom. The introduction to start class, during and after the class, Mr. B made time to meet, greet and include me in class discussions. He even asked me about my goals and direction. To hear the educated responses I provided, I could tell Mr. B was surprised when I told him my age. After class, Mr. B gave me a male's perspective about life and even some of his experiences. Once I told the professor about my challenges, he explained how he was also ridiculed a lot in school until he successfully made it to college. It brought my attention to Mr. B's facial features which displayed spacious gaps between all his teeth and I knew that was a feature to be ridiculed for. Kids are cruel. He continued by confirming the nick names they pinned on him about his teeth. He was bullied harder the older he got but his smarts was his fuel to grow pass them all. Mr. B said he knew he was going to become someone great as a result of his humiliation. He told me if he hadn't experience it, he may not have become the great professor he was. I was so glad for our talk. I knew that being mislabeled as being soft or gay which was what a lot of young men went through even the highly educated Professor B. I was 12 years old listening to a well educated black man's point of view, giving me a positive man-to-man life-lesson talk that identified with my own struggles. It was dynamic nurturing that once again my precious mom had caused to happen and I still value it to this day. Those were some of the riches she provided for me.

Both of my Grandfathers Relationships weren't much to talk about as male role models. I can't remember any input from them at all. After hearing the educated updates of my mom's family history it helped me to dissect the real reasons for Papa's impartiality!?

I flew back to Ca for my Grandma Mae's funeral with intentions to take care of all administrative preparations which I knew my mom would still be trying to do. I told mom to let me serve, and I wanted her to let go and mourn and she was very grateful. These are the times you show your parents the rewards of their investments. I busied myself handling all matters at the Church, where I had also been bullied, but this was about Grandma Mae's home-going Celebration. For a long time I'd witnessed mom being that take charge person for the family. She coordinated so many family functions from front to back because it was her passion, even down to ensuring all the photos were taken. After two full days of preparing, I began to see in her eyes, mom and I were long overdue for one of our valuable Relationship talks. This quality time could only take place after all of the formalities and hopefully before my return to New York. Right after the life celebration of all the friends and family galore was over, of course, mom discovered more covered up family history. Grandma Mae had always vented to mom all things and stuff told to her and during her last months of illness there was a release of information Grandma wanted mom to know, yes more secrets about family ties Grandma Mae needed to expose! Believe me, I felt it would have been okay to just tell it and set it free. My dad's side of the family did the same thing at funerals too. I guess it was just the traditional way many families choose to be. Why? Mom said the reward was to finally see with your own eyes, she was just grateful like me to have already received the missing pieces to complete her life story. We both laughed out loud, WHY? Why do we feel the need to hide things? I guess there is always something in our life time we all will wish to take to the grave with us!?!

I'd long been encouraged by so many friends, mom included, to use my writing skills in some form or fashion. A book, lyrics for songs, poems_movies_ pushing me to show my talents. The real question is will I ever get this book completed? I am working on it. Every time I hear mom ask, "how is the book coming", I think about all the years I have let more of my energies be side tracked by all the distractions of what young people do. I live in New York! People!!

These journals are my rough drafts originated from back tracking my life journey and the many different conversations with family while listening to lots of unfortunate situations with all my connections. The hardest part to writing comes when deciding with caution to mind-map everything into a meaningful story line. Everyday we see how the internet communicating is misconstrued, even when you tell the truth! Who said the truth will set you free? I, like the one liner, "You Can't Handle the Truth!" That was an understatement! Family!!!!

My mom's prayers have been my road map for all my successful travels. She laid the ground work when I was young. The only thing missing for me was having a closer Relationship with my little sisters. I was elated to finally have contact with one of my sisters, now living in close proximity to New York. Mom was right again, my sister and I are all grown up now with the power to make our own choices. The blessing is being able to choose again after time gone by. To finally find each other and still crave the Relationship that we longed to keep as children, is now possible and a beautiful thing. We are beginning all over again, this is the allotted time for us. I keep reflecting on what mom meant when she said, "I wish you could see with my eyes!" God has appointed all chapters of our life, we have to be patient and wait for it. When we were younger it was not the time for me to be involved or caught up in the life their parents chose. I am not to even question Why, but I am just glad I get this opportunity now. Being in this present time, given the opportunity to greet one of my sister's and her family is priceless. My Relationship circle is broadening with rebuilding some set aside kinship. I've met the nephews I never knew I had. Relationships, I am richer than I even imagined!

Watching my mom start and complete her selected goals and then still be determined to equip herself with even more positive Self Improvement Training has moved me to redirect my energies again. I will stay focused to forming an outline to write my book. Mom has achieved many accolades for her hard work; achieving the highest Economist Award a Civil Service Recipient can receive. Her aspired driving force has always motivated me more. She exposed me to each of her lessons taught in 'Relationships Training' to become certified as a Relationship Educator through a Christian based school, and I was excited for her and to be her understudy. Then she told me "Let's take the Notary Public plus the Real Estate Document Signer Certification course together" I was pumped that we could have a connection in different states. The document signer was an indefinite certification, to keep it in affect, you had to keep the Notary credentials current. This opened up additional doors for me in New York with fluid benefits which were astronomical. My mom! It impelled me and opened up the space I needed to write, I have began again to write with renewed passion. Living in New York expended the many distractions all around me. I am young and still full of passion to party. I had to master keeping my mind fueled to sustain the levels of urgency and determination required to live here comfortably. Once again, unknowingly, my mom provided for me with solutions all the way from Ca. I tell her over and over again, "Thanks mom, I love you".

Thinking back I never jumped at the opportunity to seriously write, I chose instead to help other people with Resumes, Business Memorandums, orchestrate lesson plans or outlines, teach young adult Bible Study classes incorporating self help plans, family obituaries and some song writing all to add with my administrative titles of employment. My journals, consists of listing various Relationship circles from my young life to present for the study of people to background the main objective in order to formulate the big picture of Relationship trails to create the story. Reader will need this to understand how the dots connect or be in suspense of how the story ends.

I remember a very special relationship with my Aunt Ru, I think she knew that she was my favorite Aunt. She was so close with my Mom and always a part of our life from my beginning, she took me with her to hang out with her high school friends at park settings and lots of other places in her Sirocco, Volkswagen a great gift given to her from a sincere uncle. She was such a cool and loving Aunt. The exposure my Aunt provided me was so impressionable and also attributed greatly to my development.

Aunt Ru, kept order in the chemistry of my sharing and playtime with the other kids, riding my tricycle and hanging with her school friends. We all lived together in same house when I was a young approaching my teens, that to was great family flavor. While her new husband was out to sea, mom and I were happy to help when ever she needed it with her then little man. Both mom and I were so happy for these rewarding Relationships. Relationships are what mold and make us, we can't erase that we are the products of our environment. We are what we consume at an early age.

When you meet people and have conversations with them, you first remember, people are what they devour. So we shouldn't be quick to judge, all people you meet will soon show you what they are made of. Why should that ever be a problem? The problem comes when we feel their worthiness is ranked with God. You have to know and remember that God never looks down on anyone, his love is unconditional. People! Please! We need to get it right with God, and no time like the present, don't run out of time, do it today!

What one person lacks another person will be abundantly gifted and the reason is to learn from one another, at least where it deems permissible. It has taken me a long long time to get here but my mom always told me, "No one is better than another, we are all different. God made us all unique for his purpose, not ours!" It brings to mind a little sermon that I actually gave at church when I was approaching my teens, 'The Makings of a Fool, Any One Can Be One'. There will always be people who make asses of themselves and still look down at others. "We have to be quick to forgive in order that we be forgiven." RELATIONSHIPS!

I am grateful for the people whose paths I've crossed, while others I'd wished I'd skipped over, I came to understand all acquaintances were an intended part of my life lessons. I have had a host of Relationships gifted me before and after I left home that I would have never experienced and I have no regrets. I've learned that most people want something you have or they will need to drain your ear so just be a silent listener for their stories. The in between for you is, to hopefully, have close family ties or extended family who will truly be there for you. To grow into a man, is a huge lesson in itself. If I've learned anything, I can still build with the gift of choice but it better be with caution and exceptional choosing. Life is what we make it! It can only be enriched with God's hand, we can't do anything all on our own. To choose again is hoping we have learned what a gifted tool it is. Making mistakes is inevitable, but when you turn around to choose again irrationally, well_ it is setting oneself up for failure. In my daily walks living from Florida to New York, I still run into people who choose to be imbecile, but for me I'm still learning how to make better choices for myself. Whew!! We need to have some bad experiences with Relationships in order to recognize all the great Relationships in your life. I am very blessed to say I am so rich with good Relationships from California to Florida to my now home state of New York. That is not saying I haven't had my share of bad ones because I have in all states. The choices I've made has been to purge out the bad ones, mom can elaborate on a few of those crisis. When I needed advice about women I would ask a seasoned woman's opinion whom I could trust. I get it why my mom kept on telling me, "I wish you could see with my eyes", she just wanted me to have the early insight about life's crap so that I could channel it wisely and not crack up or give up like a lot of young men do. I do understand why God made women as help mate for the man. Support, nurturing and holding us up is all needed for success, most of us men think we can do it all on our own. Maybe a few men think they can but if you look at those few closely they aren't complete. I had the pleasure too early in my life to have met the right one for me and never found one to even come close. The world's virtues and values are changing drastically and you can easily get caught up in life of disorders with wrong influences. There is always a way out. The future is scary when you can see that people are trying to rub out the teachings of the Bible.

CHAPTER 4

RELEASE (Bring it all to surface and give it to God)

Jean is completely astonish over the perpetual pages of journal authenticated by PJ. Particularly it's content. It solidifies how God's hand is always working. She can't believe how similar their conversations are, when in all the time it has taken, she had been perplexed with what to say or how to put the writings for this book together. Jean had began writings long before she even took PJ's laptop to Best Buy to get the password off to open and download his files still too sensitive to want to look at it all. Almost two years later to be guided to insert some of PJ's journal together with his Mother's language to tell of his journey and his legacy of overcoming bullying. Careful not to change his notes they hand selected his thoughts so you can know PJ intimately. Truly in his own words. Imagine how powerful it was for his Mom to read and release for more healing. You will read many of his own words are identical to her earlier writings. She has learned a lot more than she ever knew from his journals. Two years plus, Glory to God!

Jean reflects on the joys of motherhood when PJ was a baby. The joy that comes in the morning is her daily comfort now. All the messages of scripture that had fed her over the years have come to be real for her life. When PJ died, Jean believed she would never ever be able to mend her pain. This feeling holds such personalized trauma. Her definition of pain she defines as, Pulling Apart Inner Nerves! Thru all the therapeutic photos of PJ, it was evident that he was selected and sent by God to enhance and embrace Jean's life so she could fully spiritually develop. Jean realizing all those times she would be saying to PJ, "I wish you could see with my eyes", was not even cluing her to realize that her own eyes were covered. PJ had started very young with a multitude of experiences and he was triumphant in doing his best to hurdle them all. Jean knew he was gifted but the bigger picture was that he became all he could possibly be in spite of so many people tugging at him to pull him off course. It all molded him into a person with no fear, and he could see clearer than she'd ever hoped. Jean was ecstatic to have been a part of his life.

Sitting in silence recalling so many blessings, Jean visualizes PJ, age 3, saying to her "Mommy you need to go to church". "What"? Jean (smiling now) at that age she couldn't believe he would say that. PJ never wanted to see his Mom unhappy, as a little boy, he knew the spiritual 'main ingredient' to provide his Mom with for inner peace. Jean knew it was time for her to slow down from her party mode and focus on one of the most important roles in life, being a Mother! Jean's own attentive Mother Mae, felt the need to encourage her to go out and meet new people to not be so consumed by PJ and single parenting. When PJ told his Mom to go to church, the impact of it was instantly effective, it served it's purpose. Jean didn't stop her partying immediately, instead it was a gradual process and she finally slowed it way down. She made PJ a promise and never broke it, they started attending Church with her Mother and family every Sunday. Jean could see this had marked the beginning of God's already predestined journey for them both. Many times family members will forget the importance of Relationship ties until something happens and even then, people still don't comprehend the intentional lessons to grow from. We should learn how to enhance our vision as we carefully take life-steps (one foot in front of the other) to arouse spiritual proportions. As we all travel the roads of life and come upon the sink holes and trenches, it is vital to be somewhat prepared for it can alleviate those typical questions that surface whenever crisis hits, Why? or Why Me? All our life-journeys are in the order intended by God. To put it another way, … "Our personal intentions don't necessarily coincide with God's preordained plans! Our daily purpose should be that we concentrate on getting our individual selves right with God!

Give thanks to God every day for your Relationships, they are all designed with significant purpose and intention. Reverberating her pass 65 + years, Jean knows how fortunate she is to have the rich experiences with family and very special lady friends.

"I always thought my son would be the one running to my bedside in a time of serious illness. It is imperative for all to take heed, it is not wise to assume your life plan is yours, but to be conscious of every precious moment in time. Without hesitation say and do things that are most important to you. No one knows how much time is left, no matter what age. God has every one of our Life-Steps ordered from birth to ending. Be determined to be the best possible person you can be today and each new day you are granted! Most importantly, never forget your FAMILY. Teach your children their family history. DNA and explicit details of who's who. Take serious note, when you rub out any part of your family tree, you bring destruction upon yourself, that becomes a loss for you. No matter what your personal feelings, be careful not to rob your children and their generations to come from knowing who they really are."

Why so many people today try hard to plan lives without spiritual insight comes from the lack of spiritual knowledge from their parents and grandparents. Spiritual knowledge is vital in order to have balance. The newer generations are showing the inescapable results, we now visibly see the changes. Situations all across the media display the results of extracting God's word. Do we really believe that all is well, is it human nature to walk blindly into the future, consistently running into brick walls, stumbling in the dark?

Long before Single Parenting began for Jean and 5 years into her first marriage she made a choice. It had been a fragile marriage appeased with love but flooded with substance abuse. The time to separate was crucial and the chance to get both her and PJ's life back on track. This was a significant turning point for change. Jean's only concern during this separation was determining what was best for their 3 year old son. She already knew it would be hard for everyone involved, yet it would be better for PJ to grow up enjoying both his parents in harmony vice tense opposition. Realizing the absence of marriage would attain the aura minus conflict, then separation was necessary. She was not implying it was the best thing for PJ, but because of the differences of lifestyles, it would definitely be healthier. Jean admits his intentions were good but by then, it was much too late. With all the love PJ's Dad continued to express, the chemical abuse overpowered him and he soon realized Jean's request to divorce was wise and he was quick to add "but, until death do us part". Jean said he didn't know the en-depth teachings of the Bible at that time but she knew more. His Dad's love was genuine for all his children. Jean had once hoped all the promises and rehab would've been successful and could have kept their marriage together. Jean chose to never disclose any of the Dad's life style to PJ until he had grown into an adult, or if he questioned the details. Mom and both sets of grandparents taught him how important family was no matter what the circumstances. PJ's half-sisters were, one sister before his Mom and Dad married and two little sisters after their divorce. PJ's Dad only married PJ's Mother, Jean. It wasn't until PJ was grown that he and Jean finally had that talk about why she chose to separate and later divorce his Dad. Jean didn't think what consequences would be by staying silent. For PJ it brought about verbal contamination and fabrication. Explaining after the fact to PJ why people choose to fabricate/Lie is usually because they have unhappy lives, not worried about who gets hurt in the process. It should be taught early that lies lead to more lies and soon that person forgets what they've said. PJ had carried around these scares too long. Jean was happy now that PJ is finally getting the answers she never knew were crucial directly from his Mom. Thank God for another blessing. Communication and Understanding are so vital for any Relationship in order to grow strong. It is important to have honest communication with your children as early as possible. We tend to give what we learn and if it stunted growth concepts we should be ready to fix it. Clearly show your offspring that parents are human and capable of mistakes too. Jean hears her Mom saying repeatedly, "I wish I had it to do all over again, knowing what I know now."

"Whosoever shall give to drink unto on of these little ones, a cup of cold water...he shall in no wise lose his reward." (Matt 10:42)

Jean had shown a lot of strength over the years because she never once discolored PJ's dad in any manner. She only prayed with intention in her heart that it was the right thing to do. Both of PJ's parents always expressed love for one another and especially towards PJ. They knew they were young and mentally unprepared for parental responsibilities and marriage. The main ingredient of God's word was missing from both their lives, they were blind and destined for catastrophes. Jean recalls the trip to PJ'sdad's funeral. All the family and friends had gathered with the exception of his three half-sisters. It was such a relief to finally talk about all these things now after all the years had passed. It rejuvenated PJ to finally hear the actual order of events that brought him into the world. To really love someone is to let them go and because of all that had happened, it really had a double meaning for Jean.

Jean felt so bewildered to think of how long PJ had carried this deception of false information around with him, it was heart breaking for her. PJ had always despised a conscious liar, he'd learned early with his upbringing that it is also a choice people take. As an adult his feelings about grown people choosing to lie, turned him off indefinitely. Looking down in her lap with a blank stare, Jean says, "It just feels good to look back on some earlier decisions I made for our lives and be blessed to see the results and know it was the right choice! There are no assurances when a person makes a decision that it will turn out to be the right one. Something PJ use to say to Jean, in her financial stress filled days of bill paying. "Mom, you make the choice and hope for the best and always Pray for the rest." Oh what Joy he brought me!

Jean talks a lot about her mother (Mae) and how she was blessed to learn so much from her. The restoring for Jean is to witness PJ's journal writings which also exposes a lot about their Relationship in his own words. Amazing! Jean recognizes all the lasting lessons awarded from her mom, something imbedded in all of Mae's children and they still cherish the lessons. Remembering one of many statements her mom would say to her during kitchen table discussions, this was while Jean was pregnant with PJ, "Let your children always see Love in you to learn that it is what made them and that same Love will fuel and power you through all your circumstances"! PJ told his mom he remembers them all being together in joyous camaraderie. He summed up this had to be after Mom and dad were separated and that's why it had him so confused. His memories of Mom and dad around him were of genuine love and friendship. Jean let PJ know it was genuine and automatic, they both wanted the best for him. His dad''s battle with drugs was huge and he loved us enough to let go. Their long awaited discussion of family history while sitting in the middle of a huge collection of pictures helped PJ to revisit many occurrences. It was an epiphany, PJ knew if he had missed this opportunity, he would have continued to live unhealed. When given the missing links of your life and your eyes are uncovered you can experience a true healing. Jean was tearful but humbled just to revisit it all. Family history is vital and due to today's technology anyone can find their ancestral history by DNA. The added bonus is when the human factor of actual names and stories are included.

PJ still reminiscing over the last few visits he had at dad's place, seeing him looking tired, depressed and not as lively. The people traffic still in and out, but there was something different in the atmosphere. Noticeably, his dad's whole behavior had changed from the uptempo, playful and happy attitude. He recalls his dad telling them he was going to be a better dad and fight the drug trap and that he was sorry it broke up his marriage. Another awakening for PJ of why he was confused about all those Relationships. PJ envisions that his dad must have had health issues then but he just thought it was the drugs. PJ told Jean there was so much happening at dad's place that he spared telling her and Jean just reached out and hugged him tight, grateful that he survived all of those visits. She knew why PJ and dad's girlfriend had dissolved their Relationship connection due to a string of lies which all took place a year before his dad's passing. Jean was happy just relieved they had this emotional, cleansing. Thank You God!

A powerfully spiritual event happened for Jean at X-husband's funeral. There is Bible scripture on how married/divorce is clarified where people are not free to re-marry except for adultery or death. During the funeral precession it was the first time ever, that Jean felt a true disconnection from their marriage. They had already been legally divorced about 6 years but PJ's dad always stressed to Jean he never considered their marriage terminated. The power of it all took hold when PJ got up to speak at his Dad's funeral, which we all had no idea would take place, but his words capped it all off, it was a priceless and unforgettable moment in time. Jean saw a strong young man (age 13) before her eyes and felt confident that PJ had really grown up using his spiritual tool belt for life. Like so many funerals, it always seems to happen, the unveiling of hidden truth. Exposed at the destined time and still so devastating and shocking. Jean knew only all the family members and braced herself for meeting all X-husband's friends and neighbors. They all seemed to know who Jean was and very anxious to approach and convey information with her. Of course it was way too much information all at once, but that entire stay in N CA is where Jean received validation, His dad had laid to rest in peace while still carrying a strong love bond for PJ and Jean, he had always expressed his love for Jean and PJ to all who knew him. 'Unconditional Love is what God teaches us, it is Forgiveness.' PJ knew his mom, had long since, forgiven his dad but at that time he just didn't know the story. It was a healing for PJ to meet all his relatives, ones that he never knew he had. it opened up his ethnic heritage ties, a major moment for him. This whole experience taught Jean to pull her strength from deep within because this is what it really takes to do everything for your child. Experiences in life are not to stunt our growth, instead, it is to help us stand on our own two feet. When you get knocked down in life, get back up, brush yourself off and maybe next time you'll see it coming and duck!

There are people who actually steal their own identity by falsifying who they really are. Amazing! Be careful not to fabricate your journey just to please others. When we are blessed to have children it is a second chance at ensuring they don't get knocked down by the same obstacles of challenge that their parents had from peer pressure. Be very careful parents not to rob your children of their true identity and dreams. NO ONE in this world is perfect.

When Jean's mother Mae finally sat down with her to share her detailed life story and it's hidden secrets, it was at the intended time. Jean appreciated her Mom's story in her adult age and realized that things happen in a certain order for a reason. It is in the order God intended and never ours to question. Without Biblical insight you won't have the insight intended. Don't block your opportunities for a better life, pick up a Bible.

People are locked into thinking their journeys need to appear flawless for on lookers when being true to yourself is the only way to grow upright. Jean was glad to know her mother's full story. The love of her mother and how she was raised only made Jean appreciate and love her mother even more. Her mom dealt with every obstacle laid before her like a champion, that is what made her ideal and courageous. Her mother was the strong unmovable Christian for her children, grands and great grands of whom some will never realize their gift. Jean got up and walked to another side of the kitchen reflecting on the past, when she turned around she said "I am humbled to have been given the gift of this particular Mother in my life, I sincerely Thank you God"!

To have experience bullying was the course intended for PJ and his parents. Jean identifies with her son's agonies of growing pains, his more compounded than hers, but she knew it was easier to have had similar experiences to be able to help teach her son the ways to overcome. To stand back and recount events helps Jean to see with uncovered eyes! This Life Lesson all adds up to being given the correct tools, then implementing those tools daily for molding inner peace and new found strengths in order to stand up against most challenges of life to make it easier to come through your journey and reap the rewards. It's a big picture but it is what it takes and she witnessed her son PJ doing just that all of his blessed years here on earth. It is a serious parental responsibility to feed your children the antidotes required for whatever demons that hover around them. Parents must first uncover their eyes and see their needs and be courageous to fight for a solid and firm foundation under their feet and let them fulfill their dreams. When you become a parent it's no longer about you, so get over the "I / Me" syndrome! Jean's mother taught PJ so many impacting things, Jean recalls coming to to pick PJ up from her mom's and he had learned his first song which he sang to Jean right when she opened the door. PJ was 2 1/2 years old, "You Are My Sunshine". Momma Mae told Jean while she was pregnant with PJ (disgruntled by hubby's life style), "You'll never know true love, until you have a child"! Deeply this still touches Jean's heart, as more tears roll down her face, it was a precious moment, Priceless!! Whenever you give a testimony, it could impact and give insight to someone else and help them make better choices. This true story is not intended to short change anyone, its purpose is only to help many with insight with the excellent tool of choice.

Currently there are still no valid reasons why anyone is subjected to the horrid evils call bullying. PJ's intentions of writing his own book one day was in hopes of helping anyone with their personal Relationship experiences. Since he has been laid to rest, Jean understands the blessings of getting his lap top and discovering his own personal journal writings, she says and I quote, "I can only write this story from a, heartbroken, Mother's perspective, knowing partially what his intentions were".

Jean retraces when PJ first decided to write, he toiled with the fear of being judged even more. Back in the early 1990's he tried explaining what future technology would be capable to take devious measures to outrageous levels. PJ informed the few who listened, how it would heightened bullying to unbelievable epidemics. People could then be inconspicuous and inject aggression tactics to people of choice. The bullies will be legally disguised to control people's minds over the internet. Jean remembers her astonishment and recollects how in a way, it had commenced at her job site. PJ had foresight! Our eyes were covered and just couldn't fathom future headlines, it was unforeseeable it could get to that extreme. She was amazed, she felt with PJ's foresight that he was going to end up in politics or journalism writing about projected news headlines. PJ's concerns were valid! Once he discovered his parents had even experienced bullying in the worse way, it empowered him differently to circumvent his reoccurring evils. It seemed to refuel him with new vision to face all challenges, head on. All of the predestined women in PJ's life were a blessing of help, they created the right atmosphere for his impressionable years. The results proved rewarding, PJ was clearly a young man ahead of his time and he knew exactly what he wanted to do in life. His adrenaline was always about making a plan to achieve his goals.

To witness your child transform out from under the entrapment of being bullied is uplifting and memorable. The determination to battle through so much of it, afforded PJ amazing results. He was spiritually gifted with intellectual phenomena. PJ made a lot of good choices all through out his life which allowed him to experience his life long dreams. He grew to understand how the fibers of life are intricately woven and each one is tied to the twist and turns in roads traveled. The stream of achievements accomplished during PJ's 35 years would have not been possible had he given in to the bullying concepts of given up and believing only in himself. Instead he chose to replace Pain with Perseverance! Jean was overjoyed and grateful that they were both blessed to have many family and friends as prayer warriors. They all walked with her through PJ's entire journey of life and still to this day show her great love.

Everyone who knew PJ were reassured of his brilliance. His mom knew he was always in good hands with God's protection! PJ consistently told his mom not to worry about him, but he knew it was her biggest pass time when he moved so far away. For Jean, writing this book has blanketed her with a healing like none could have believed during that day in January 2015. Just reflecting over it all doing her best to convey pieces of PJ's life experiences in a book has been phenomenal. PJ always wanted for his mom to unlock her workaholic state of mind and start enjoying life more. He joked with her a lot, he use to tease her about letting down her brick wall to let a good man in. Fortunately, PJ was around to observe an interested gentleman caller who approvingly and properly received his mom's full attention. This gentleman was a member of the Church of Christ too. PJ confirmed this to be the best possible start to a Relationship for his mom. Jean uncovers her eyes to see the wisdom PJ unfolded throughout their lives together as she lets go to feel her healing take over.

"Ask, and it shall be given you; seek and ye shall find; knock and it shall be opened unto you." (Matt 7:7)

Jean professes, this was the confidence PJ always carried with him. Too long, Jean had covered her eyes in part, but to see the proof of how PJ was covered by God, is major life-lesson in itself. Now it is Jean's turn to leaf through the collection of pictures and achievements left behind from PJ's life to display the memories from start to finish.

Jean wants nothing more than for anyone young or old hurting from the stains and pains of bullying to know they can get through it all with

God's help. Don't stop to allow someone else to dictate your position in life. Know that you are uniquely created for a purpose, God's purpose. You will always have Love, the Love of God! Believe in yourself, you are unique and special, specifically created by God.

"Blessed are they which are persecuted for righteousness' sake: for theirs in the kingdom of heaven." (Matt 5:10)

"There is no difference between the Jew and the Greek: for the same Lord over all is rich unto all that call upon him." (Rom 10:12)

Looking through tear stained uncovered eyes, she can see years of life lessons with some she missed. Jean is cognizant that PJ was given to teach her just as it was intended, PJ IS my God send gift.

The lessons of life are easy to miss, but when you look through uncovered eyes, it is very plain to see. Let's all practice at keeping our eyes uncovered!

I pray from reading this story it will help any to Rewind, Recall, Release so Restoring can began. Only then can you recognize how blessed you really are.

CHAPTER 5

RESTORE (Relationships uncovered!)

More than two years has gone by since PJ has been laid to rest. Jean revisits the first time she was blessed to experience a real life-like dream of PJ. Phenomenal! So incredible, better than words can describe, she was comforted and rejuvenated by each one of her dream experiences. Jean felt like all she wants to do now is sleep, hoping to have more blessings of sweet dreams with PJ. This is a true definition of a Dream Come True! God continuously works in all our lives. To sit back and look at the big picture, God had been working wit Jean since the beginning of her life towards restoring her for this horrific time, incredible. He has the master plan for everyone at all times! "I will go before thee, and make the crooked places straight." (Isaiah 45:2) Jean will give a few synopsis from many different occurrences as she witnessed God's help through all these particular season of her life. Her eyes were uncovered! She rejoices in the evidence that prevailed! God is good, all the time and all the time God is good!

"And it shall come to pass, that before they call, I will answer; and while they are yet speaking, I will hear." (Isaiah 65:24)

1. God sent Jean an Angel to be at her side the third day of the first week, she was sitting in the Hospital cafeteria. Pasha was her name, she sat alone in the cafeteria eating soup and reading a book. Jean approached Pasha and asked if she could sit with her. They began to talk and share why they both were there. Jean describes their union as divine. It was destined, they were instantly connected by God. Their harmonious new friendship was like none other. They both knew why their paths crossed. Each one of them had special men in the hospital with same symptoms and the only difference was Pasha's husband had been there already for six months. With uncovered eyes, Jean witnessed Pasha's Faith in God's plan and her magnificent strength. Pasha and her daughter were at the hospital daily so Jean now had a new praying family. Once Pasha knew Jean's complete situation (husband and son), she became a new found committed, caring and nurturing friend in every way. Each day they saw one another and became more and more acquainted. Pasha also told Jean not to worry, she believed that since PJ was young it would give him an advantage of successful recovery. Jean thought to herself, how unselfish this new friend was to give her hope, in spite of what her own challenges were. Pasha wanted to meet PJ and with urgency. Jean felt God carrying her through this overwhelming emotional time and seeing Pasha so concerned, she knew it was evidence of God's work. Pasha's husband was under ICU care and she explained why there would be no opportunity for Jean to meet him. Jean felt a bit swayed that she couldn't do something to lighten Pasha's heartache. They would sit together daily, counting their blessings to each other and praying. They both realized the magnitude of God's gifts, Jean became aware of how much she was missing her husband and family. Seeing also, how much it had helped to have had her sister and niece there. Relationships are powerful and necessary. Meeting a person like Pasha and all the comfort she provided getting through those remaining days of PJ's life, UNFORGETTABLE! God sent an Angel who has become a life long gifted friend. After a week of Pasha's display of faith, trust and strength she encouraged Jean to return to CA and see about her husband while PJ was doctor described, in recovery status. Advised by Pasha not to worry since she was at the hospital daily. Jean was in awe, she pictured a halo over Pasha realizing this was a true servant for God. Evidence! Jean had to make a decision. Pasha could see the concerned look Jean wore, then dominating evidence kicked in when Pasha assured Jean she would check on PJ without fail, daily in Jean's absence. Pasha continued by telling Jean she would call her to let PJ hear his Mom's voice in the mornings on her speaker phone. Jean filled up with tears, she understood the urgency that Pasha had displayed at the beginning of their friendship, protectively wanting to meet PJ. That wasn't strange to her at all, while PJ was growing up people were always fascinated by his involvements and wanted to know him. Now look at PJ, even on his sick bed the ability to draw folks in was still working. Yes! Jean's religious belief of witnessing, first hand, the power of God showing up in all her places of crisis, busily working! Evidence! Jean knew she would want to give testimony about PJ's story.

Restoring was all over Jean as she recollected all of these amazing accounts through it all. Jean pondered a moment, reminiscing how she had been told repeatedly, what a treasure Jean was given to have a son like PJ. To hear Pasha offer such a service could only be that of a genuine Christian. Recalling that moment in time in PJ's hospital room when Pasha met her son, was spiritual, it seemed as though all the hospital noise stopped leaving a smoldering light all around PJ and Pasha. It was a union, without a doubt, comforting to all three of them. "Restore my Spirit Lord, it needs Restored!'

"And let us not be weary in well doing: for in due season we hall reap, if we faint not." (Gal 6:9)

They all held hands and Pasha prayed. Hallelujah! There is no words to describe it, God's presence was in that room. Jean felt so comforted by this angle of God. She was refreshed with new strengths, this is what it took to get Jean to CA to return with intended help! God's order is amazing, his blessings were enormously with her at all times. The gifted new friend Pasha, her attentive concern and out reach towards Jean and her family. Priceless! It was Pasha who saw his eyes light up to hear his Mom's voice over her phone. Jean reflects and "Pasha is an amazing Saint! I just love her". It was a total of three very significant calls. Jean stopped for a moment in silence and said, "I will never close my eyes to the blessing of this wonderful woman Pasha who took time away from her own life crisis, to serve a God that loves us all, ensuring I had that precious time with my son, she was proof that our God sends angel to our rescue and I Thank God with all my heart!" Restore my Spirit Lord! Pasha displayed the love that she unmistakably carries for God. Our world would be so great if we had more people like her who serve unselfishly. Another life-lesson in plain view, which Jean witnessed with uncovered eyes.

2. Miss Mil was a very good friend who Jean had lost contact with over the years. Mil was fluent in Spanish and now resided in Florida. PJ actually looked her up while living in New York and reconnected Jean with her good friend 5 years earlier. PJ and Mil shared the same birthday. Fast forward to PJ's collapse, the minute Jean called Mil, it was like there had been no time lost, she was shocked to hear the news but ready, willing and able to assist Jean with whatever she needed. Mil did all the translation between PJ's family and Jean whenever requested. God selected Mil long ago to cross paths with Jean for all their fond memories but especially for this particular aid and comfort. Wow! Restore my spirit Lord!

A quick three day turnaround and right back to hospital. There could have been so many things to have prevented that to take place. Jean kept her Faith lifted because it was God at work!

"Thou I walk in the midst of trouble, thou shalt stretch forth thine hand against the wrath of mine enemies." (Psalm 138:7)

Jean let Go and let God. With tears flowing, she continues, retracing the love efforts, God shows her daily. Jean being blessed to returned to PJ's bedside was important not to miss. She comprehends the order of things most important, PJ and his Mom's still sharing time together, a Restoring process granted by God.

3. So many things have transpired over these two years of missing PJ. Jean confirms she makes a conscious effort to keep her eyes uncovered in all that she experiences in her life now. It took a while for her to get to this understanding, and Jean's awakening of God's plan for her has been inspirational. Her husband, family and all her special friends have provided her with more than she'd ever expected. Everywhere and all around her she has been blessed with love from all who knew and loved PJ. Jean found herself getting back involved with the Cancer Resource Center where she had volunteered since her 2012 Retirement began. The atmosphere, great people and work ethic had always been rewarding in itself. This also helped to jump start Jean's healing process. Restoring….. God sent lots of angels to visit with Jean and they came right to their home with powerful gifts, evangelic spiritual songstress spreading God's enlightenment, gift baskets, money and testimonies of their life experiences which helped Jean see she was one of many hurting and learning how to heal.

Jean had many expected loud outburst in the first year, just getting some of the pain out. Her husband understood her pain. Jean felt bad that he had to experience so many outburst for they came unannounced all hours of night or early mornings and startled her husband many times. Private Bible study was and will always be vital for her ailments. Jean admits that some days she may forget but when she gets up early in the mornings with her prayer time and Bible study, it always brings on a great peace that passes all understandings. Her joy comes in the morning. Restoring...

Within one year's time after PJ's death, God made it possible for Jean and her husband to strategically relocate to a new area. This was a reluctant decision but it made so much since to just get away in hopes it would ease some of the pain from most of her implanted memories. It really didn't matter where they lived because her son would forever remain a memory in her heart. Jean knew she had to initiate the work of healing which, for her, mainly required studying the Bible and reading a lot of self-help literature. Receiving the blessings of life means there will be reasons for all the different seasons, all of it being in God's intended order.

Jean's husband spoils her by making many comforts for their sanctuary where ever located. The Ca home was awesome and a great memory. It is better to have loved and let go, than never to have loved anything at all! If you are blessed to keep living, life changes are inevitable. Being able to both be retired with adequate retirement incomes is a big blessing also! Jean is grateful that she retired when she did because it allowed her the gift to spend much more precious time with PJ than other wise. Restoring,.... Jean and her husband are relocated and both doing the simple life where peace is everywhere they look. Her husband's craftsmanship has afforded them a beautiful new dwelling with low maintenance plus the economy is unbelievable in AZ. They have made a few friends of choice and attend a Church of Christ right in their community. The new season of their lives is gradually blossoming with fragrances all finally rewarding to engulf.

4. Believing in the spiritual power during these times can be very confusing without guidance. Jean recollects her repetitive verbiage to PJ about how God was teaching him to stand on his own two feet from all his growing pains. She recalls their surprising awareness to discover his peers admitting to PJ that he had too much knowledge for someone his age. That was crazy reasons for the continuous mental and verbal abuse from his peers. PJ wanted whom ever had to experience any type of demoralization to know that his Pain Perseverance taught him to push through it and you will go forward to eventually pass up all the haters. He wanted to embed in victims to adhere to the tough hid it creates with faith that you can grow up with the power to move on. You have the gift of choice. These bullies will not be in your life, the rest of your life. Believe in yourself, your strengths and identify with other victims to collaborate together. Our purpose is always to help make someone else's life better, why not make that a task of outreach to cure what also infected you. Never let anyone control your feelings, when you react to their foolishness you give the bullies control. Those were my PJ's words to share with like victims of then and now.

Jean reminisces how she would always help him through by telling him first how much she loved him and then turning up the painful tough love. She wanted desperately for PJ to learn how to resolve his problems with his spiritual life tool belt. PJ finally accomplish mastering inner peace but with a tough exterior hid, sometimes too tough. He had zero tolerance for stupidity. Jean was always right there, ready to run the race with him to the finish and that was how they were for each other. Her own tormented bullying from adolescence to adulthood gave her experienced insight to help PJ through his. We may be products of our environment but it does not classify or dictate who we choose to become. Being misread is a common error, but when a person is gifted with spiritual confidence, you can watch bullying become amusingly digressive and give you back control of your life. You will uncover your eyes and start to see the Bully is also a victim. Pray for them to find the answer.

Jean learned the hard way to never take sides with PJ's peers because they had all took advantage of her soft side.

When Jean stopped rationalizing each bullying incident, and instead listened with uncovered eyes to PJ, she felt so disappointed in herself for missing so much, she confused his being an only child with the early stages of bullying. PJ had legitimate pain from constant torment over the years. Although Jean knew this hurdle was necessary for PJ to work out for himself in order to become stronger in the cruel world of peers. She blindly wanted his development to evolve the same way hers did and just as her Mother had shown her. PJ' results in his adult life developed into an independent fearless individual. The reasons for our different seasons will make us or break us. Jean restores knowing she gave PJ the correct tools to work with. Jean restores knowing PJ was never rebellious. He had the love of Jesus, God our lord and Savior as his blanket repellent from a very early age! Hallelujah. Jean's consistent quiet prayers for PJ's outcome were about the development of a strong individual who could take on the world without fear.

"All things, whatsoever ye shall ask in prayer, believing, ye shall receive." (Matt 21:22)

5. Re-visiting a particular day at church, while in transition to bible class PJ was being challenged as usual from his class mates, all of his past bullying incidents had brought him to that moment in time, his breaking point. Right there in the church parking lot he exploded. He stood up strong to a routine bully as Jean walked up with a few ladies to witness it all. PJ was now exuding with confidence, he had NO MORE tolerance for bullying. Priceless! Using all his gifted insight, PJ put that bully in his place that day. He had finally figured out how to deal with his demons using the word of God with pose and intellect. Jean was blessed to witness PJ's victory, and because of God's grace, PJ received positive feedback from all who were there. He had been gifted with rejuvenated fuel to excel and grow forward being encouraged to never look back. After this incident PJ eventually chose to go and find his own spiritual dwelling as Jean remained his biggest supporter. PJ was 14 years old when Jean allowed him to make choices for himself. PJ had reached his full mental development at a young age, which made it easy for all who knew him, to recognize how brainy he was. PJ had unforgettable qualities; assertive, confident, with zero tolerance for liars and haters. Jean took him to night College with her when he was 11 years old to show PJ life after high school would be about his own choices. He was so motivated to know later in life he could make his own choices, no more force feeding.:)

6. While still restoring…. Jean has ample room to identify with God's master plan of gifting her PJ's 35 years. Inevitably, PJ was predestined to come into his own confident man from all of his trials. Educated in full capacity to know who the true judge is and taught how to put on the full armor God with benefits! This is what PJ's biggest rewards in life came from! An accomplished individual, not flawless, but so applaud-able!

Restoring…… Jean, was baptized into the Church Of Christ in 1983 experiencing the awakening of her purpose of serving in many ways all the steps ordered and intended for her life. Reminiscing Jean revisits another scene with PJ age 4 saying, "Mommy pray about everything, don't worry about anything". It was her early days of single parenting days of financial stress. Once little PJ said this, it immensely assisted Jean to accept that she had another Father in life, Father God! Having PJ in her life aided her to learned this.

"My God shall supply all your needs according to his riches in glory by Christ Jesus." (Philip 4:19)

She was privileged to be chosen to parent this particular gift of a son. He came into Jean's life and taught her all about the Power of Love. If you are a parent or aspiring to be one, know the importance of fueling your life's tool belt for your child's journey. Jean's prayers are that all readers will connect with others everywhere to share this story. The blessings will flow forward from this book.

7. PJ and Jean talked a lot about life, from current events, politics, religion, family, and more. Being his mom she had learned over the years how to talk to PJ without debating the issues. She learned to be a good listener for him which lead to better understanding of respecting another person's opinion. This is something a lot of people never learn how to do in order to establish better communications. Whenever or where ever PJ received this type of consideration it was easily returned to others.

With these new technologies of communication a person never knows how the receiving reader's frame of mind will be. We see it all over the media today, misinterpretation. They had long ago talked about the how dangerous the internet would become. Jean expresses how they were brain storming together regarding his great upcoming book of projection. PJ was always motivated when he and Jean spoke about his ideas. Their talks regular conversations also included topics from Jean's, Relationships Education, surveys to probe at the 'why people are hurtful' to others. Jean says, "Parents, there comes a special time when your children mentally grow up, it is crucial to sit with them and have Truth Talks, and not lie to make yourself look good." It is important for parents to help their children understand how the choices made in life are what dictate their journey. He wanted to know a lot about his Dad's family, PJ had wanted to know if his Dad had any experiences of bullying? That one question alone opened up a lot more information for Jean to enlightened PJ with. Answering PJ's question, "Yes" his Dad had those same experiences growing up and so had she. Restoring, …..the healing in knowing that Jean had the opportunities, in time, to talk about and answer the late, almost too late, questions all before PJ left this earth.

"I am the bread of life: he that cometh to me shall never hunger: and he that believeth on me shall never thirst." (John 6:35) Restoring……..!

It is better to have Loved and Lost, than to never ever have Loved at all! Hallelujah, Amen! Jean was blanketed with a soothing feeling of knowing PJ was the blessing for her life and the memories are what continues to sustain her and they are endless.

8. Jean rethinks over one of the Relationship Classes she completed in acquiring her certification to educate others. Her instructor discussed how they'd all seen it in other people or themselves, where people fabricate their own life stories to feel whole. The instructor continued expressing to the class, that the down side was people tend to eventually really believe in the fabrication. Jean said she and a girlfriend took this class for self-improvement and preparation for marriage. It was the course Spiritual Innovations of Prepare & Enrich, and they were recommending it to everyone. Being a licensed 'Relationship Educator', License #1217906, which Jean says she acquired to enhance her own life choices and share with PJ, resulted in helping them both see the character of people much clearer. It is dynamic prerequisite for better understanding the many relationships one encounters. A Mother and son's Relationship was their starting topic and they dissected that one to the core. It was a great book writing connection for them which opened up many new topics of discussion concerning Relationships that were enriching and empowering.

People tend to run from the requirement to effectively communicate which consciously or unconsciously pushes away many important and/or intended Relationship experiences. Jean restores herself daily recalling so many good memories with PJ, another was when she asked him one of her Counseling questions that so many people had failed, "How many Relationships do you have? Jean was always convinced of PJ's brilliance and he was one of the few who immediately understood the question. Thru Jean's Relationship counseling, several people had missed this question by thinking it made reference to only romantic Relationships. Wrong! There are far too many different types of Relationships.

The first should be your Relationship with God and then the others, for example; Mother to Son, Son to Father, Sister to Sister, Aunt to Niece, Uncle to Nephew, Grandma and Grandpa to all the Grandchildren, cousin to cousin, etc. With all of that being the focus, the most essential of all is our Spiritual Relationship in order that we be granted the enriching ones. As PJ expressed it, 'The Main Ingredient'! If this Relationship is off balance then their will be great turbulence throughout the rest of our lives. PJ felt strongly about the future luring people in to severely misuse the internet concept. Back in the 80's PJ's peers had unconcerned foster parents and it displayed the neediness in them, and he felt this would no doubt, lead to misuse of the internet concept. A dangerous but realistic concern that has now become prevalent. Wow, PJ really knew what was up and coming. So to the masses especially young people, know this, be anxious for nothing, only God gives the increase.

"Blessed are they which do hunger and thirst after righteousness for they shall be filled." (Matt 5:6)

Jean's true blood line was now revealed to her because this was the intended time. "It was Already in the Order Intended by God". The intentional delay to tell Jean was directed and requested by her Dad who had actually been her Step Dad. He had taken full custody of both Jean and her oldest brother when they were very young. Once he married Momma Mae, who had two children, he wanted his entire family to carry his name, persuading Momma Mae to never tell them different, another family Secret. Why, Jean recalls while looking back over all those years and thanking God for his order, had it been in any other way, it may have been disastrous, especially since it was compounded with all her very own experienced bullying. Momma Mae and Step Dad were the best parents, their dynamics and firm direction, during her adolescent years, displayed an unquestionable richness of Real Love, Courage and most importantly Understanding. While growing up, Jean never understood her oldest brother's rebellious demeanor and it wasn't until right before their Mom's heavy illness took hold that she made it all clear for Jean to understand the whys. What a courageous woman both Rue and Jean agree, a powerful life lesson to be blessed with her legacy in spite of her journey traveled. God blessed her richly with a husband who came and helped her to travel on in her journey sharing, caring and baring it all together.

Restoration has been all throughout their lives together as Jean resonates over all that PJ pushed pass and through to become the extraordinary man that he is within the 35 years granted. Just to name a few; he learned to let his ill feelings towards the evil doers slowly dissolve and his numerous achievements began, teaching bible class, giving a mini sermon at the age of 9 in C.O.C., playing piano by ear lead him to arrange coral groups for musical plays at his middle school with accolades, he lead and directed church choirs, obtained leading roles for Balboa Theater Company, and he was selected for major roles in the "Russian Ballet, all acquired prior to age 14. After turning 16, his adult achievements were his mission accomplished! His writing skills afforded so many accolades, he worked for Qualcomm, Children's Hospital, Office Manager for several Corporations in Southern Ca and Fort Lauderdale, Florida, Microsoft Office of New York, and certified business owner as a Real Estate Loan Signing Agent and Document Signer. He obtained his Bachelor of Science Degree in Business Communications in 2008. These are just a few of PJ's achievements noted to make it visible to all who's struggles in life vary with mistreated experiences. You can use whatever is thrown at you for fuel, to serge through life with confidence that you can attain your passionate desires but the blanket of strength to wear has to be the word of God. PJ's project to write his book was the reason his mother was inspired to put his story out there knowing his writings would have truly identified with commonality towards today's victims. Knowing PJ would say to the young and old alike, "Don't be pulled into the pit of thinking you are not special in your uniqueness, you are already gifted with something to offer this world, that's why we're granted the privilege to live! Live,….. persevere and, one day tell your story"! You never know who you can save.

Jean can now reveal her personal identity, I Jean, am the Author and Mother telling this true story of the amazing PJ, which has helped me to arrive 2 ½ years later, to stand upright again ready to help where ever I can. I work hard daily, remembering to keep my eyes on the prize where all my blessing flow. I am so grateful that in the midst of writing this book for my son PJ, God revealed to me everything I'd ever want to know about PJ through his Laptop computer. It allowed me to insert 'In His Own Words', a small portion of his book notes. Yes, there is so much more that he had to say about everything and everyone but it is all for me to decipher, and as his mother, I also have all my questions answered in the time intended. To all of you who have given a loved one back to the rightful owner, especially, if an only child, I pray this book will help you in ways you would have never considered before.

PJ's legacy is his complete walk of life, a victim who was fiercely bullied but chose to rise up above the contamination to prove to other victims you can still succeed with yours dreams. Believing in himself was the goal he reached with help from a few who truly loved him, not to exclude, a lasting Relationship with the eternal Father, God.

"He that over cometh shall inherit all things and I will be his God, and he shall be my son." (Rev 21:7)

This book is an outreach to the many existing victims affected by bullying and mistreatment from any Relationships.

Printed in the United States
By Bookmasters